The Bartholomew Effect:
Awakening to Oneness

Larry Vorwerk

Two Harbors Press

Two Harbors Press
212 3rd Avenue North, Suite 290
Minneapolis, MN 55401
612.455.2293
www.TwoHarborsPress.com

www.awakeningtooneness.com
Larry Vorwerk
P.O. Box 401
Northfield, MN 55057

ISBN - 978-1-935097-76-1
ISBN - 1-935097-76-8
LCCN - 2009942966

Front Cover Illustration by: Brian Netten, www.nettendesign.com

Editors: Barbara Krause, www.makingwordswork.biz; Nita Wolf

Back Cover Photo by: Paul Krause, www.dancingsun.biz

Typeset by: Peggy LeTrent

Printed in the United States of America

Acknowledgments

This book has been a lifetime in the making. As a person who questions life and reality, I gained knowledge by talking with and observing others and experiencing life. These were the elements that contributed to my evolution. Many people played a direct role in my life by sharing their awareness, wisdom, and knowledge of books and other mediums. All of this enabled me to write about what I understand to be true.

I acknowledge my parents, who are no longer living in this world. They were religious people who truly believed in and demonstrated their faith. Over the years, they instilled a firm foundation in me that included acceptance of things beyond the five senses. They were loving and caring parents. Although my beliefs were different from theirs, I still admired them for how they lived and treated others.

I appreciate the academic background I received in all of the sciences, especially in the natural sciences. This foundation has provided a deeper understanding and appreciation of nature. My wonderment of creation has encouraged me to seek more answers in order to understand three monumental questions: Who are we? Why we are here? and Where are we going?

It is through relationships that we grow. A relationship that offers challenges and conflict provides an opportunity for reflection. Because of my first marriage, I started to read self-help books, focusing on related areas of learning. In the process, I came to know myself and am grateful. This marriage also produced three children for whom I am thankful.

It is through harmonious relationships that growth can be the most rewarding. My second wife, Nita, has journeyed with me over the last fifteen years while my life exponentially unfolded. I relied on her encouragement whenever I doubted myself or felt vulnerable. As the initial editor of my book, she spent many hours going over the concepts and offering various perspectives. Her contributions made the material more readable and understandable.

For these reasons, and for so many more, I acknowledge that without Nita in my life, this book might never have been written. I am appreciative for all that she has done for me and for all she means to me. Nita has truly brought growth, joy, and love into my life.

I am also grateful for the contributions of numerous people who have played essential roles in my life. To them, I say thank you for your influence and contributions to the person I am today. Without your encouragement and support, I might not have written this book.

I acknowledge my professional editor, and our personal friend, Barbara Krause. With growing interest in the subject matter of the book, she brought clarity and professionalism with her final editing of my material. She definitely helped make the process of compiling this book both feasible and rewarding.

Several groups continue to be influential in my life. One of these is the Unity spiritual center that we attend. Two other gatherings that are special to me are the Spiritual Transformation Group and the BE Group. I have met with them for eleven and six years, respectively. I celebrate the Oneness of these like-minded people, from whom I have gained so much. Truly my spiritual family, they have offered joy, love, and wisdom over the years.

My final acknowledgment is for all of the support, love, and inspiration I have received from Jesus the Christ and other great teachers from the Other Side. This support fueled my multidimensional life experiences, insights, and ever-growing awareness that became the foundation for this writing. Without experiencing a higher reality, this book might not have evolved. With gratitude, I thank you for speaking through me and for all that I Am.

Namaste,
Larry
2009

Letter to the Reader

Dear Reader,

A deep, driving desire inside continues to nudge me to promote the message: *We are all One.* As you experience this awareness while conscious in this world, you will naturally strive to work and live for the good of the whole. Most likely you will realize your inseparable bond with the Divine and experience an intense emotional feeling of Oneness with others. It is my hope and intention that my writings will ignite this spark of awareness in you.

In this book, I share my personal journey of spiritual evolvement. I recognize that my experiences are unique. Your journey may be similar to or very different from mine. The Bartholomew Effect, a culmination of my journey of profound insights and experiences, is what I will describe throughout the book. Historical accounts of Bartholomew, one of the Twelve Apostles of Jesus, are limited. It is stated that Bartholomew worked with the land before joining Jesus and the other apostles. Later, he was persecuted and put to death for his religious beliefs.

In simplest terms, the Bartholomew Effect is a pure, unconditional love relationship that I now experience with Jesus all of the time. Although you may know this relationship by a different name, I believe the Bartholomew Effect can be experienced by anyone when the timing is right for growth of the soul. You will learn the details of how my relationship with Jesus has evolved.

I speculate that this relationship may be the reason why the apostles were so devoted to Jesus. They were able to tap into this pure unconditional love of Oneness that Jesus emulated, and I now experience. This connection is tangible and is a significant part of my self-realization. Throughout the book, I have used italics in passages that indicate the words of Jesus.

My book is not just a Christian story. Readers of all spiritual and religious persuasions can find meaningful food-for-thought. This pure, unconditional love relationship is much greater than one group's cornerstone on the Truth. I will describe how you might evolve into Oneness with all living things.

Oneness has many levels of intimacy. One example is that you may feel you have a unique, unspoken connection with another individual or with your pet. Perhaps you can go into higher levels of consciousness or realms of being. At an accelerated level, maybe you experience an energetic vibration that naturally merges souls together into Oneness. Pure unconditional love between any soul and another living thing will create this effect.

To explore Oneness, you do not need to duplicate my personal experiences. Oneness develops more through spiritual maturity and a sincere readiness to explore a deeper purpose as a human on this planet. Why are we really here? I believe we are here to represent sparks of the Divine as we journey back to the Source of all that is true. It's all about perception and projection. We are to be the Light of Truth for the planet and for all those around us.

I do not consider myself to be elevated, special, or in any way set apart from you. I face many of the same human challenges as you do. At times I have to deal with other people's poor choices that affect me. I face health issues and challenges that give me opportunities for growth by working through them, keeping me humble. I can get overwhelmed with the stress of a busy schedule and personal responsibilities. What I have learned is that deep faith, persistence, and coping skills have helped me to overcome adversity. These strengths are what see me through to more peace and harmony.

By reading my personal journey, contemplating it, and trying some of my suggestions for exercises, I hope you will gain insights to your questions and personal challenges. Through intention, you will grow and thrive. It is an ongoing process of continuous learning. New insights continue to come to me as I experience an expanding awareness into Oneness. We can live a spiritual life within our day-to-day dramas when we focus on one moment, one day or one quantum leap at a time.

For over thirty years, I have been writing about this message of Oneness in my personal journals, often sharing them with friends. It is now time to share my writings with you. My work has taken many shapes: poems, meditations, prose, and spiritual journaling. Throughout the years, I've questioned all aspects of life and have now reached the point where I see a direction that is right for my high or true self.

As you experience and learn to live this Oneness of Love that you are, you will become a co-creator with God and other enlightened individuals. Increased awareness will help us get in tune with our higher selves, establishing a better world on earth.

Namaste, *
Larry
2009

*Namaste, originating from the Hindu culture, means, "I behold the Divine in you as I behold the Divine in me."

CONTENTS

Spiritual Insights

Throughout my life, I've come to realize that certain spiritual insights are important to a successful, joyful life. You may want to pay special attention to them as they appear throughout the book.

- Our imagination is one of our greatest gifts.
- Our greatest limitations are the limitations we put on ourselves.
- Living life with the realization that we are One is the key to emotional well-being.
- Our intention is the most significant key in manifesting our desires.
- Our intuition is our constant connection to God/Source.
- To feel is to live.
- Our perfection, our love shared, is our eternal Truth.
- To live life without masks is one of the most freeing things we can do.
- The world's wisest, most benevolent souls come into our lives.

*O*ur imagination is one of our
greatest gifts.

Chapter 1

Blind Faith

By keeping an open mind toward everything, listening to our intuition, and then acting on it, we begin to live life to the fullest.

Hindsight provided a new perspective. In my mind, I was the only real contender to confirm or deny the adventures of my childhood. As I looked back on my early years, I realized how I was strongly influenced by my parents' steadfast and compliant belief in Catholicism. These were good people (who are on the Other Side now) who wanted their six children to accept and practice all the tenets expected of a faithful Roman Catholic family.

    We prayed regularly to our statues of Jesus, Mary, and Joseph and to an assortment of angels and saints. Almost every night, before bed, we would say the Rosary sin, and you could go to Hell if you attend another church other than the Roman Catholic Church." That was the end of the discussion. After all, none of us dared to *think* about going to that horribly hot Hell, nor did we want to float around on some sort of gray cloud, called Purgatory, until someone prayed enough to release us.

I thought I was different from other children, including my siblings, because I never went through the typical rebellious stages. I was a compliant, easy-going, introverted child. Even though I didn't always agree with my parents, I usually felt that they were doing what they thought was best for me. I always respected and appreciated their genuine love and concern for me. Only later did I realize that my religion was effectively controlling and allowed for little deviation.

In contrast, my earliest spiritual experiences in nature were considerably more expansive. I spent a lot of time in nature by myself and believed (and still believe) in its magic. My inquiring mind pushed me to explore the secrets of life. Nature, in all of its forms, gave me many opportunities to discover new horizons. This was my true, personal and sacred time.

We lived in Iowa, along the Mississippi River, and our city had beautiful parks near my home. With a myriad of places to explore, my days were spent observing the details of the smallest creatures to admiring the vastness of the night sky. In those days, I had more questions than answers about nature. It became a driving force in my life, and eventually, it became my career. Nature inspired me to think inquisitively.

Compared to many youth, I probably led a sheltered life. My family had only one car, and six kids did not easily fit. In actuality, I had never traveled more than twenty-seven miles from my home until I was a junior in high school. I rode on a school bus to a track meet outside of town. Looking back, I was content with home-based life.

In the late sixties, however, I decided to leave home to attend a university in Iowa, taking an opportunity to spread my wings. It was freeing to find other students who shared similar interests in biology. I also met students with common religious beliefs and joined the Newman Club at the campus Catholic Church. This was a setting where we, as young adults, could come to know each other in a Christian environment. For the most part though, spirituality wasn't high on my list of interests while attending college. It was more about learning to come into my own, breaking free of parental influence. It was a time of fun and academic learning.

After graduating from college, I was one of the fortunate students to be able to find a job in my related field of study. I became a zookeeper. This career followed me throughout my entire adult life.

In the mid-seventies, I married someone who shared my interests and studies in fisheries and wildlife biology. I continued to be involved in traditional Catholic religious practices, and my wife converted to my faith. During the earlier years of this marriage, I moved away from the conservative aspects of the religion and ventured to the fringe of Catholicism: a charismatic branch that I attended for six months. Among other practices, I experienced hands-on healing and speaking in tongues. At some point, I began to feel that the charismatic group was not as fulfilling as I had hoped. Also at this time, my wife felt threatened by charismatic practices and wanted me to stop worshiping with the group. These negatives convinced me to stop being involved with the group; however, deep inside, what I had experienced definitely expanded my thinking.

In the late seventies, we moved to Minnesota where I became a zookeeper at the Minnesota Zoo. As we settled in our new community, I became active as a Samaritan lay minister in the local Catholic church. This ministry lasted for the next ten years. Samaritan experience helped me become more aware of our similar needs and desires, regardless of age. I was much more conscious of individual needs beyond the fundamental basics: feeling loved, being valued, and having a meaningful life.

Over the years, my innate curiosity grew as I searched for answers about relationships and scientific pursuits.

This was more of a quest for me as my marriage became increasingly challenging. I realized that my wife had escalating mental health issues when our family grew to three children. It was very painful for me to recall that I was a battered husband, and that my children experienced emotional and physical abuse. Because of my religious belief that one stayed in a marriage and did not divorce, no matter what the situation, I held on to hope that things would change.

In the early eighties, I created a prayer and affirmation that I've said daily for many years. It has become my constant companion. It became a powerful force in my life and has truly given me spiritual direction.

Dear Lord,

Please guide me in acquiring your love, wisdom, knowledge, understanding, compassion, strength, and feeling at the fastest rate that I can handle. Enable me to grow at a faster rate day-by-day. For this, I pray and thank you.
Amen.

In 1982, I experienced a totally overwhelming feeling that lasted approximately one month. For the most part, this time in my life still remains a mystery. Although words cannot fully describe the strong level of feelings and emotions that came over me then, I will describe it as a feeling of total peace and serenity.

The catalyst was the convincing feeling that my life's purpose and mission had been completed. It was time for my soul to pass on to the other side of the veil. This did not make sense to me because it was a contradiction to what was really happening in my life.

I had journeyed through much chaos and turmoil in my home, moved forward in my career, fathered another child, and was heavy-laden with the unending responsibilities of being a husband and father. I was clearly immersed in life. So strong was this peaceful feeling that I could not ignore it. I was confused. What was happening? I was completely perplexed.

Something was changing within me, and I had no one with whom I could discuss this strange feeling. Obvious to me now was that after this intense month ended, there was a definite burning desire to know my life's purpose and mission.

For two years I asked for guidance to learn of my life's mission—all with no satisfaction. An answer came to me one night when I was in bed, reading a book. Suddenly, an all-encompassing or direct knowing seemed to permeate all cells in my body simultaneously. A message that I already seemed to know came to me: "Your mission is to find emotional healing within and then bring emotional healing to people who come into your life." This directive appeared to be such a stretch at the time. I was never told how to accomplish this mission, so it was up to me.

Meanwhile, my relationship with my wife was incrementally falling apart. I requested psychological help for the family, yet there was no follow-through on this until several years later. I continued to feel responsible for my children's well-being and safety.

During this time, my only opportunity to self-actualize was to read lots of self-help books. This turned out to be the means for deep insights. I believe now that I was divinely guided to follow a path that promoted personal growth. Through my reading, I became more spiritually and emotionally mature and centered.

At one point, I was in my local library, and a book literally fell off the shelf in front of me. No one was close enough to cause this to happen. *Strangers Among Us* by Ruth Montgomery lay at my feet. I picked up the book, took it home, and began to read it. It was then that I learned about "walk ins." As I read more about this phenomenon, I realized that it was a possible explanation for what I had experienced a few years earlier.

I understood a "walk in" to be the process of two souls exchanging places with each other. Usually the soul that left the physical body felt its life challenges were too imposing to overcome. This soul exited the physical body, leaving it fully intact, and moved over to the other side of the veil. The incoming soul from the other side of the veil

Our greatest limitations are the
limitations we put on ourselves.

Chapter 2

The Greatest Gift

By sharing what I have experienced and learned, I offer a broader and deeper knowledge of reality, so that the whole spectrum of its potential meaning becomes approachable and conscious.

1985 was a significant year for me. It was the year that I became interested in reading books on a wide variety of spiritual topics. My journey began in the library when I witnessed the book, *Strangers Among Us*, literally fall at my feet. The books I read included everything from Eastern Philosophy to Modern Physics. For the next ten years, I couldn't read enough, quickly enough. Generally reading a book a week, I searched for answers to these important questions: Who are we? Why are we here? Where are we going? Up to this point, I knew that my limited belief system was just that—limited. To explore unchartered territory, I needed to stretch my boundaries.

It was during this period that I decided to write my life's blueprint. One of the books I read offered what I thought was some sound advice. It stated that one needs a firm foundation and a blueprint before building a house. These ideas made sense and could be transferred to personal growth as well. Having a firm religious foundation and then developing a life's blueprint would be advantageous for optimum living. This was an admirable goal, and I embarked on my life's blueprint.

I found that this thinking and writing process has served me well over the years. I read and continued to research those first important questions. I also questioned the firmness of my religious foundation as I continued to update my blueprint annually. I wrote about self description, my blessings, and my goals. Eventually I listed my impressions about reality. Creating my blueprint caused me to reflect, leading me to understand that I could live proactively and with greater purpose and direction. Referencing and updating my blueprint continues to be a rewarding endeavor.

Developing a blueprint for your life might be just the right step for you to take now. I suggest you do this to move from being a passive reader into exploring your own foundation and blueprint. The purpose in presenting my life's blueprint is two-fold. First, it is an example of how you might find answers to those critical life questions.

Secondly, it will give you the opportunity to get closer to Oneness by getting to know me on many levels. Then it is your turn. Completed with intention, this exercise will help you break down inherent barriers to Oneness. This process does increase your vulnerability. At the same time, it also allows others to see themselves in you. What a gift!

You will see that we actually have a lot in common. Truly, we are not that different from each other.

Larry Vorwerk Life's Blueprint

Part I Things to consider: How I Describe Myself
Part II Things to consider: Blessings
Part III Things to consider: Goals

Part I
Things to consider
How I Describe Myself...

1. Am easy-going, calm and relaxed; more a Type B person.
2. Am well-balanced, but slightly leaning toward introversion.
3. Tend to balance the best quality of life with the least expenditure of energy.
4. Am energetic and a morning person; almost always have my mind/body in motion.
5. Enjoy the simple things in life; take time to "smell the roses."
6. Control my emotions, most of the time.
7. Am somewhat passive, but assertive when it is important to be so.
8. Usually take time to figure out the likely outcome to an action before engaging in the action.
9. Do not express my emotions in a highly-visible way, even though I feel I have normal feelings and emotions.

10. Enjoy being with people, especially when we have things in common.

11. Realize that the concept of my focus expands. I create my life circumstances through thoughts and intentions. My thoughts and intentions take form more quickly, as I learn more about manifestation.

12. Am very open and honest with my thoughts.

13. Enjoy close and extended family ties.

14. Love all forms of nature and am kind.

15. Have an unquenchable thirst for knowledge and development of wisdom.

16. Am persistent and consistent in my actions.

17. Am analytical and logical, most of the time.

18. Demonstrate sound financial management.

19. Enjoy spending time with others, as well as by myself.

20. Have right-brain dominance.

21. Use vision and imagination in my creativity.

22. Am a self-taught philosopher and mystic.

23. Am practical, most of the time.

24. Believe in a holistic approach to life.

25. Am usually cautious, but one who enjoys trying new experiences.

26. Prefer to be viewed as a Cultural Creative individual, rather than a Modern or Traditional person.

27. Am dependable and of average intelligence, with the curiosity of a child.

bring light to all those we encounter. Our souls and our love for each other are eternal, for we are a reflection of the great I AM.

3. Other spiritual partners and friends in my life who make this journey Home to the Godhead a joyful, rewarding and loving experience.

4. Loving, wise and spiritual parents who profoundly influenced my life.

5. Our collective, five healthy children and grandchildren who bring great joy to our lives; each of them is honored and loved.

6. All other people who have entered my life and shared their wisdom and growth. They have given me the opportunity to love and serve them.

7. A healthy body and mind.

8. A challenging, rewarding, and enjoyable zookeeper position at the Minnesota Zoo.

9. A country where one has the freedom to express many personal beliefs and lifestyles. By being honest, sincere and freely opening my life and thoughts to others, I welcome others to share their lives and thoughts with me.

10. The ability to value people as equals, honoring their position, gender, age, race and standing in life.

11. The decision to listen to my intuition which helps me to trust individuals and situations.

12. A special home on ten acres of land where I can grow a large garden and maintain a wildlife area with a half-acre pond, trees, prairie, and wildflowers.

13. Time spent running 41,000 miles over thirty-eight years of my life, once completing a fifty-mile run in seven hours and eighteen minutes.

14. Enjoyment of the "flow state" experience during the majority of my regular runs across the landscape.

15. A college degree and profession that has given me comprehensive knowledge and understanding of a lot of the sciences, especially the natural sciences, including wildlife and plants.

16. Ways in which one can grow in knowledge and wisdom, especially through books and other individuals.

17. Creative imagination, for I realize I can manifest that which is my focus.

18. Reality experiences as I awaken to who I am, by means of the out-of-body experience, the dream state, mystical experiences, and increased communication with all life forms. This includes communication with the plant and animal kingdoms, spiritual guides and other humans who have passed to the other side of the veil.

19. Support of community at our Unity spiritual center, the Spiritual Transformation Group, and the BE Group that meets twice a month at our home.

20. Nature and its beautiful expressions of life.

21. Creativity that I express in my wildlife paintings completed during the winter.
22. Courage to write and publish my story, *The Bartholomew Effect: Awakening to Oneness.*

Part III
Things to consider
Goals of Personal Development

1. To continue in the daily repetition of positive affirmations, prayers, and directions to influence my subconscious.
2. To eat a balanced and nutritional diet.
3. To practice Qigong and other movement exercises on a daily basis.
4. To stay current in my professional literature and related subjects.
5. To continually update my life's blueprint.
6. To become more assertive in some areas of my life (the Universe presents opportunities that allow me to work on this).
7. To pray for and accept full abundance in all areas of my life.
8. To take time to nurture myself and know that I am loved, so that I will be whole and better able to give to others.
9. To continue to learn and grow in all ways

10. To become a better listener, focusing on others.

11. To increase my speaking and writing abilities.

12. To acknowledge my weaknesses and mistakes in life, learn from them, and never let them diminish my self-esteem or self-love. "In order to love others, first love yourself."

13. To acknowledge my "shadow" self and accept it as part of me; learn to improve myself by working through it.

14. To meditate on a regular basis, always acknowledging and expressing gratitude for blessings.

15. To experience life by focusing on feelings, becoming more sensitive to the feelings of others.

16. To review my dreams daily, learning from them.

17. To continue to develop my intuition and to be responsive to it.

18. To keep an open mind regarding communication, so that I may always grow.

19. To regularly read books that supplement the categories of my book list.

20. To place high priority on peace, harmony, love, joy and a passion for life as I work in my profession and live life.

21. To create new experiences of Oneness through my thoughts and intentions, knowing that giving and receiving are One.

22. To continue my spiritual journey Home by awakening to who I really am, LOVE: an expression and generator of this emotion.

23. To achieve ascension in this lifetime, to pass beyond the cycle of physical life, to express a full conscious awareness of the love that I am, in the higher dimensions of reality.

Things to consider
Goals of service to family, community, and all of life.

1. To emotionally support Nita by prioritizing open communication and nurturing time, showing that I love and value her (bring her a rose, write a little love note, compliment her).
2. To be the best lover, spiritual partner, helpmate, and friend to Nita.
3. To emotionally support and be a positive influence on our adult children and their children through open communications; write or call my adult children at least once a month.
4. To feel joy and fulfillment as I work with Nita in our gardens, later sharing our harvest with others.
5. To continue to raise the vibration of our home and acreage by communicating loving, nurturing thoughts to all living things on our property. In this way all who visit our home will not only feel and experience this loving energy, but will also contribute their loving energy.
6. To remain connected to our communities.

7. To do all things with love in my heart and compliment several people each day.
8. To serve as a lay counselor, opening my high self to others as I assist them in their spiritual growth.
9. To continue collecting information from my wisdom questionnaires, personal contacts, internally-received wisdom from spiritual beings and wisdom gained from life experiences.
10. To be of service to all people.
11. To lead, support, and participate in the BE Group and in the Spiritual Transformation Group, continuing to fulfill my spiritual mission.
12. To show unconditional love to others, even when that love is not returned.
13. To bring Christ Consciousness to earth by demonstrating it in my daily life.
14. To help others experience the feeling of Oneness and unity with each other and with all living things.
15. To continue to work on my mission—my passion—to help others with their emotional healing by helping to bring Oneness to earth as we ascend with the earth into the fifth dimension.

$\mathscr{L}$iving life with the realization that we are One is the key to emotional well-being.

Chapter 3

New Perspectives

One purpose for physical life is to have the opportunity to change and develop thoughts within the natural law of cause and effect while under the illusion of linear time. In the higher dimensions of space, it is believed that our thoughts are manifested the instant that they appear in our awareness. Since time in the higher dimensions is the eternal now, where the past, present, and future exist at the same time, we do not have the same luxury of changing our thoughts before we experience the effects of those thoughts. So it is important to remember and develop our highest thoughts while we are in the physical world.

After finishing my life's blueprint, I started thinking about writing a book on wisdom. During this time, my children and I were visiting a special person at a nursing home. My children's grandparents lived in another state, so this was a way for the children to experience a relationship with a senior citizen in our area. Although their "adopted" grandmother was ninety-six years old, blind and had few visitors, she always seemed happy and had a lot to say. I thought she had gathered much wisdom in her long life, and that there should be some way for her to share it with others besides the few who knew her. I felt that her wisdom was her Light to the world, and, as such, might be extinguished without the opportunity to pass it on to others. This gave me the idea to gather wisdom, enabling others to learn from each other. I would simply ask people to complete a wisdom questionnaire.

"Understanding what is true, right, or lasting; common sense and good judgment" is the definition of wisdom as defined in *Webster's New World Dictionary*. All of these aspects of wisdom resonated with me and continue to be a strong interest of mine. Today's world needs more wisdom, yet I realize that no one knows all the truths of wisdom. I felt compelled to gather collective wisdom. Each of us is a spark of the Divine—a part of the whole of God. If I pulled together the most concentrated nuggets of wisdom from a diverse group of people, the passages would demonstrate interpretations of how God speaks through people.

I planned to compile the wisdom acquired from a "million years of life experiences" by collecting information from people of all ages, gender or sexual preferences, and backgrounds. If the average person completing the questionnaire were fifty years of age, then 20,000 people would be needed to complete the collection.

Maybe, dear reader, you would be interested in contributing your wisdom. Please see Collection 1, "Wisdom Questionnaire," at the back of the book and submit your responses to me at Larry Vorwerk, P.O. Box 401, Northfield, MN 55057. Another option is to complete the questionnaire at my web site, www.awakeningtooneness.com. Answers to the wisdom questionnaire remain anonymous, so you can be open and candid.

Between 1985 and 1994, I was aware of a real growth spurt. During this time, I had some unique multidimensional experiences that changed how I perceived reality—they certainly broadened my thinking. Being a natural scientist by profession, I began to search the field of modern physics for answers. I tried to find where the explorations of spirituality and science met. I realized that my religious background was no longer adequate in helping me to understand who we really are and what reality is. Too many of my questions were not answered adequately by religious dogma.

At this time I still practiced the Catholic faith, yet felt uneasy about all of its doctrines, rules and beliefs. In November of 1988, as a final effort to search more deeply within the Catholic Church for answers, I embarked on a pilgrimage. Twenty-three of us traveled to the little hamlet of Medjugorje, Yugoslavia, where it was reported that the Blessed Virgin Mary had appeared to six young people who lived there. These daily appearances had occurred for seven years.

The people in my group and I did experience many unusual events while in Medjugorje. I personally saw an eighty-year-old, blind woman experience restored sight during Mass. Imagine the commotion! That experience made us believers in miracles.

Two other unusual events occurred. One focused on Mary, Jesus' mother, whose presence was symbolized by the scent of roses. People in the chapel at Medjugorje claimed to have smelled the fragrance of roses, even though there were no roses in or around the church. At another time, many in the group and I witnessed silver rosary beads and chains turning a gold color, regardless of whether they had been brought from home or purchased in Medjugorje. Several of my personal rosaries and sacred medals turned gold and remained gold. Other ones, after a period of time, returned to their original silver color.

Some individuals in the group experienced additional, unexplained events. One was the vision of a lighted, thirty-foot, concrete cross at the top of a mountain. No electricity existed there. Some saw a beautiful mural of Jesus in the sanctuary; yet, upon moving closer in its direction, saw nothing. All of these shared occurrences appeared as miracles and had no explanations.

I came away from this experience knowing that even though I had witnessed many things, some experiences had a different meaning for me than they did for others in the group. I was acutely aware of my ability to use more discernment and not be swayed by others. I certainly was impressed with the possibilities of miracles and knew that perceptions cannot always be placed in neatly-tied boxes.

Our belief systems and ways of thinking create anticipated manifestations according to our expectations. Most of the visitors who journeyed to this small community, as well as the native villagers, had strong, traditional Catholic belief systems. Although once a product of that system, I did not leave Medjugorje renewed in the Catholic faith.

I appreciated this trip, and it expanded my thinking. For sure I felt the energy and sincerity of everyone there. Each of us had powerful, meaningful experiences, while standing right next to each other. These occurrences were personal and unique revelations. And, each was *different*.

There was no right or wrong about what was experienced. Many felt that Mother Mary was asking the people there to focus on their sins, repentance, and conversion to the Catholic Church to be in alignment with God. I felt this interpretation was too limiting and controlling. It revealed to me that people's beliefs were dependent on their interpretations of God and expectations of a Great Creator or Holy Icons.

This explains why some people see Jesus when they leave this physical plane through death or have a near-death experience; others, with a different belief system, may see Mohammad, Buddha, Krishna or other avatars. We create our comfort, merging with what fits into our belief systems. If we are sincere and have good intentions, we will experience something comparable.

The trip continued to stir something in me because one night, about a month later, a multidimensional experience happened to me that changed my life forever. As I lay in bed, suddenly and to my astonishment, I found myself moving from a conscious state into another state of consciousness. Amazingly, I was very calm and relaxed.

At first, one soul's consciousness literally merged with mine. What came next is difficult to explain because the experience is uncommon to most people. Often an unusual experience can be explained in terms of another experience that is universally understood. In this case, there really are no words to express another state of being. I felt an increased state of illumination and knowledge within my physical body that surpassed anything that I had ever known. Then another soul's consciousness merged with the two of us. With that experience, again came an increased state of illumination and knowledge that exponentially multiplied. I was in an all-knowing state of consciousness during this time. Without understanding how, I instantly knew the combined wisdom of higher realms of being.

This continued until approximately twelve souls became One with me. At this point, the level of ecstasy was greater than I could contain. I had to make a decision either to leave my physical body behind, as it would have spontaneously imploded, or to return to my regular state of consciousness. I'm here, so you know my decision.

This was a totally life-altering experience because I knew that in a higher state of being, we are literally One. Since then, I have pondered why I experienced such instant wisdom and knowledge. I retained only a fraction of what happened in that short time; however, I will always remember that experience. I have never read about or talked with anyone else who has undergone a similar, impacting experience. Now I had even more questions: Why me? What's next? How do I share this knowledge?

In hindsight, I realized what a gift it was to obtain such instant, powerful knowledge. At the same time, I felt frustration emerge as I returned to a human state where most of us struggle to gather basic philosophical awareness. Over the years, I searched for an explanation of that night's experience. It wasn't until much later that I stumbled upon some passages that strongly resonated with my experience.

I would like to share those passages, with the author's permission, from *The Star-Borne: A Remembrance for the Awakened Ones*, by Solara. Her words align with my thinking on the dimensions and importance of the word Oneness.

"For our next phase of evolution we must come together as One.

This entails an initiation into Oneness wherein we merge our separate identities on an Essence level and create a new state of collective beingness. In order to facilitate this, we must release our attachment to ourselves as individualized units of consciousness. This is our greatest and final attachment to duality. It is the last portal which must be passed through in order to move into the Greater Reality.

Although we have long known that we are One in Essence, we have still clung onto our identification with ourselves as separate entities. This has been entirely appropriate and necessary during our cycle of earth experiences in the Template of Duality. It was in perfect harmony with the Divine Plan that we perceive ourselves as separate from each other so we could fully develop our state of awakened conscious Oneness. (p.278)

However, to move onward into the New Octave, we must now lovingly release our identification as separate beings.

You may discover within yourself a whole new set of fears about letting go of this final illusion. You may feel that if you do this, you will cease to exist. But this is not the case; you will actually be more alive and vital, more fulfilled and radiating than ever before. And you will be much closer to the state of being which we call Home.

Oneness does not mean that we are all the same. We still bring our unique combination of energy to our star of One. It does means that our predominant reality shifts from being separate individuals to being part of a greater whole. Once again, we are venturing into the realms of the unknown. Here we shall experience an enhanced state of beingness as we unite into One vast Being. As our primary identification with ourselves as individualized units of consciousness fades away, we shall become larger, not smaller.

Our collective being is immensely vaster and more magnificent than anything we can presently imagine. Together as One, we can achieve that which we have most yearned for during our phase as separate beings. We will experience true fulfillment. This is a prerequisite for completion upon the earth plane.

Hence we are being called upon to make the final sacrifice, which shall prove to be no sacrifice at all. We are called to unite together in an initiation into Oneness, merging the family of humanity into a collective whole. Our primary identifications with ourselves shall be with the One which we truly are—you, I, and everyone else combined.

This is the quantum leap which leads us ever closer to Home!" (p. 279)

I searched for more answers that would expand my consciousness. At that time, I did not know the souls who merged with me that night. It would be another nine years before that revelation occurred. With that experience as evidence, I never again doubted that we are all One at a higher vibration.

I began to explore other forms of consciousness.

Out-of-body experiences soon captured my attention. Among other authors, Robert Monroe's books on this topic made my reading list. *Journeys Out of the Body* was the book that piqued my greatest interest.

For three years I tried to achieve out-of-body experiences. I had little luck getting beyond the stage of vibration in the spine, (as Monroe describes). I started to give up. Then one evening in October 1991, I was having trouble falling asleep. Around 3:00 A.M., I decided I would go through some relaxation techniques to enable sleep. I was very tired, yet conscious. After five minutes of relaxation, I became exceedingly relaxed and felt quite warm and tingly. The next thing I knew, I was floating near the ceiling of the bedroom.

At that moment, I knew I was out-of-body. I could see objects across the room. I didn't think about looking down and back at my body lying on the bed. I realized, from what I had read, that I had to think of going somewhere, or else I would "fall" back into my body.

At this point, I want to share some of the experiences of my out-of-body travel, questions I had, and insights gained. During my out-of-body experience, I decided to fly to a friend's house. Instinctively, I knew to put my hands together over my head. The next thing I knew, I was flying through clouds. Then I increased my speed to that of a commercial airliner. I vividly remember the moonlight reflecting off the clouds, while everything else was dark.

After a short time, I found myself at a level where I could see the fields below. Soon I was actually in a house that I thought belonged to a friend, yet was mistaken. Only moonlight illuminated the rooms, and no one was at home. One detail I remembered was the blue wallpaper with cat prints that stretched down the hallway and throughout one room. Neatness was the overall impression of the rooms, with many of them decorated by a number of figurines and other furniture.

Since I found no one, I left; however, it certainly was a new experience for me. Awakened in me was the insight that this plane of consciousness was as real as our physical reality.

This experience demonstrated that I didn't have as much control over reaching my destination as I had thought. For example, I found myself suddenly on the first floor of some motel. I ran up the stairs and then walked the second floor hall. There were other people in the hallway, but they were unaware of me.

Since I was out-of-body, I thought I might as well test some physical boundaries. My reading had suggested that I could do some things that humans could not do while in this state. I decided to walk through a wall. It actually worked! I was surprised that the wall provided little resistance. Moving through the wall felt as if I were navigating through tissue paper.

Approaching a well-lighted room, I saw a woman who was standing in front of a mirror, observing her image in a blue dress. I wondered if I could hold on to solid objects. I put my arms around her waist, yet she seemed completely unaware of my presence. Previously I had read that people in the physical world could not interact physically with those in the astral plane. This appeared to be true. Then, just before I left her room, I tried yet one more test: I decided to walk right through her. Again, my action was unnoticed.

Although it may seem that I was dreaming about this experience, I am confident that it really happened. My expanded awareness allowed me to come into contact with many new things. What I realized is that different planes of reality simultaneously exist. The state of consciousness remains the same; we are just in different planes of reality. My experience helped to confirm what it must be like for people who die unexpectedly or have a very emotional attachment to the physical world. I'm referring to ghosts or apparitions. These are the spirits of people who still think they are in the physical world and are trying to interact with those who are alive. My experience is that interaction or communication between planes does not easily happen.

Still in my expanded state, I continued to experiment. I went to many places. At one point, I wanted to leap to the future, but believe that my preconceived thoughts of the events of those years denied access to my spirit. Instead, I found myself traveling—to what year, I really didn't know. I was in a big house, similar to the one in which I grew up. After walking into a bedroom, I discovered a white and green cloth calendar hanging on the wall. The year was 1985. I walked from room to room, exploring and learning what I could in this time and place.

Eventually, I hesitated slightly in my decision to visit another location. In that quick moment, I found myself back in my bedroom. I blinked and then found myself back in my physical body. Being in another reality had been quite an adventure, and I knew that another plane of existence was as real as anything in this physical plane. That reality allowed thoughts to be immediately manifested. In this physical plane, I have the benefit of linear time, drawing reality to me. I realized then that I'd rather not have things pop into my head, manifesting instantly. Experiences in the other reality could become a wild ride if I didn't know how to control them.

As I look back on this experience, I believe our physical reality might be changing now. I think we are beginning to manifest our physical reality more quickly through thoughts and direction of focus. Many scientists and spiritual philosophers believe time is accelerating. If that is the case, it is even more important that we be aware of our thoughts and how we use those thoughts. Perhaps we are more mature now and able to handle instant manifestation.

Something else to consider is the rapid-speed electronic communications systems that are surfacing. Does the dawn of these systems help us rehearse for things to come? A myriad of possibilities that seemed too far-fetched during the 1990's now has the potential to create very fascinating lives. I realize that most people don't necessarily have a longing to search out multidimensional realities. In fact, many people tell me that they are afraid to try such experiences.

That information led me to think about my great desire to explore beyond this reality. A friend once asked me which historical figure I would choose to be. After some thought, I chose Lewis and Clark, the great American explorers. I realize now that I am an explorer and an adventurer, too. Since a great share of earth has already been explored, the next logical area is multidimensional realities.

This concept excites me more than it scares me. Perhaps I'm remembering more of who we really are — One with all. I don't believe we come from this earth. I believe we exemplify the spiritual phrase, "We are spiritual beings having a human experience." The more I experience, the more truth I find in this statement. Should you, dear reader, be uncomfortable with this type of exploration, don't worry—you are probably among the majority. I still believe that there are many dimensions to reality. We have much to explore…or rather, to recall.

Throughout the 1990's, I continued my journey. I read all that I could on subjects about self-help; positive thinking; psychology; modern physics; space and time; intuitive wisdom; psychic and other inner abilities; channeling; self-hypnosis; meditation; dreaming; out-of-body experiences; near death experiences; reincarnation; life beyond death; lost civilizations; reality beyond the five senses; UFO's; prophesy; Marian apparitions; Armageddon; synchronicity; and Christian, Eastern, Native American, and New Age philosophies.

After completing the readings, thinking about what I had read, and applying it to my experiences, I realized that I had gained an expansive education regarding who we are and what reality is. These insights are not currently revealed in our educational or religious institutions. In fact, most of these ideas are just now coming to light in the greater human community. We are on the cutting edge of a much more expansive thinking that was, up until now, somehow available only to the great masters throughout time and history.

Many books are available about the multidimensional aspects of reality; however, much still remains a mystery. Many of us wonder, as I did, what happens to us after we pass from this life's journey. I had another opportunity to learn more about this in February 1994. At night, during the state between wakefulness and deeper sleep, I found my consciousness moving out of space and time, revealing my potential future in another time and place.

I was shown and told that after this lifetime on earth, my next incarnation in physicality would be as part of a group consciousness of a newly-evolving planet. I understood that just as planet earth has a soul consciousness, sometimes called Gaia, all evolving planets have a "group soul" that enters the planet at an early stage of development. This would be similar to a human embryo taking on a human soul during the pregnancy stage of development.

I was also told that just as the consciousness of all animals of a given species becomes the soul of that species, the consciousness of a number of post-human graduates becomes the soul consciousness of a newly-evolving planet. This new planet soul consciousness is then the creative energy for all of the evolving physical creations in and on that planet.

Just as in the group mind experience I had in 1988, the energy surrounding this experience was so strong and beyond my capability that I couldn't fully go into it while still in my physical body. I did retain enough of the experience to get a clear understanding of my potential future. This could be one of many possibilities for future incarnations. Since that time, I have become aware that many of the insights I have now are actually training for this future existence. The most important aspect of my altered-state experiences points to the enlightening and broadening possibilities available in our thoughts. I wonder how many people have had similar experiences and do not talk about them. After living with these experiences for over thirty years, I feel strengthened in sharing some of them with you. It is important to act on nudges.

I have included "Meditation on Awakening" at the end of this chapter to assist you with becoming aware of your true reality: You are a part of the whole, and we are all One. This is an effective meditation to complete with another person, or alone. It is my hope that you will find this meditation supportive in your journey toward realizing your connection with all life forms. Acceptance of this reality adds new dimensions to the concept of self. Additional meditations are found in Collection 2.

With the following meditation, it would be helpful to ask another person to read the meditation to you. That way, you will be able to close your eyes and more fully go into the meditation. Also, working with someone allows you to look into the person's eyes as indicated in part of the meditation. A second option is to read the meditation to yourself, visualizing another person in your mind's eye. A third option is to listen to my audio version of "Meditation on Awakening" at my web site, www.awakeningtoone-ness.com.

Meditation on Awakening

Sit in a comfortable place and close your eyes. *(pause)* Begin by taking three deep breaths as you relax. Allow yourself to relax and release all tension and anxiety. *(long pause)* Now, see yourself as a person filled with love and ready to take a journey toward "awakening." *(long pause)*

Visualize a forest in front of you. *(pause)* At the edge of this forest, look for a special path, leading into the trees. *(pause)* With each step you take, you are able to shed a little more of the illusion of duality and linear time. *(long pause)* With each breath and step you take, a feeling of belonging fills you. You belong here. You are unconditionally holy and filled with the Creator's Light. *(long pause)*

See yourself continuing down this path through a forest glade and beautiful trees. Notice flowers and plants of all types around you. You see birds of all descriptions and beauty as they are flying and singing. Their calls cry out in songs of love and praise to you as they acknowledge you to be a co-creator with God.

A special bird lands on a tree branch above you. It carries a message just for your ears. Listen now for its message. *(long pause)* Within this forest, all are aware of their true reality. All living things, including you, are aware of their complete union with God and each other. This is the deep "Forest of the Eternal Now." *(pause)*

Through the forest canopy, you see and feel the sun beaming straight down on you. Feel the warm rays filling you with the love and illumination of the Great Creator. *(pause)* You are able to see your body more radiant than you ever imagined. *(long pause)*

Now, you see another radiant, light-filled body walking toward you from across a meadow. *(pause)* Each of you begins to quicken your pace. The closer you get, the more you recognize each other for who you really are—light-filled souls on this earth's journey. *(long pause)*

Lying beside the path is a big, fallen tree. The trunk offers itself to both of you as you sit and face each other. (If you are doing this meditation alone, picture someone beside you.) If someone is doing this with you, you may open your eyes now.) As you continue to face each other, gaze into the other's eyes. Time seems eternal as you see love coming from the person's eyes. *(long pause)* Now, see your own love being mirrored back to you in the person's eyes. *(long pause)* You are able to see and feel the other person's love, *(pause)* God's love, *(pause)* and the love of all of humanity flowing to you. *(long pause)* In love, there is no separation.

The Oneness and unity with all creation and the Creator flows in and out of you. Continue to feel this with each extended breath you take now. *(pause)* Slowly breathe in oneness and breathe out unity. *(pause)* Breathe in oneness and unity; and then breathe it out. *(pause)* This awareness of Oneness can be experienced whenever you desire. All you have to do is close your eyes and align in oneness and unity until you feel it again. Know that all else is really an illusion of separateness. You can be fully awake with your ego aligned with your spirit /soul. Only love exists. *(long pause)* Now close your eyes again as you visualize getting up from the tree trunk and slowly returning the way you came. *(pause)* You can begin walking out of the forest meadow and continuing on the same path again. *(long pause)*

Upon leaving the "Forest of the Eternal Now," you re-enter a world of linear time and duality. Yet, you are not the same. You have ignited the knowledge within you that there is really no separation between God and you, between all of humanity and you, and between all of creation and you. *(pause)* There is only the unity of Oneness; and in that Oneness, there is only love. You are loved and you ARE LOVE! *(long pause)*

Now, fully aware and awake, open your eyes and see your world with new vision.

Original, 1992
Updated, 2009

*O*ur intention is the most significant
key to manifesting our desires.

Chapter 4

Intentions

At one level of awareness we believe that outside forces (e.g. other people, the environment, or physical forces) create and control our life circumstances. When we grow spiritually and emotionally, we realize that we create our own physical reality and life circumstances. We activate this reality by the thoughts and intentions that we harbor. As we continue our spiritual growth, we realize that the best of what we want for ourselves is achieved by doing the will of God which is really our own will. This is activated by listening to God Within (or our intuition). By striving to stay centered on the spark of the Divine within us, we move to a higher level of living that harmonizes with our inner voice.

My life circumstances, up to this point, basically allowed me to grow in spiritual knowledge by reading books. I continued to struggle through life, with much to sort out about my marriage, children, and inner being. However, I sensed that I was entering a new era in life. This stage triggered meeting new people, interacting with new groups, and attending workshops that better fit my new concepts of spirituality.

My next decision was to spend a year studying *A Course in Miracles* with a friend and later with a group. This book was reportedly channeled from Jesus' words. It is widely read and studied throughout the world. In summary, the premise of this book states that we need to focus our thinking on "what is real and what is not real" and move "from fear to love" in our thoughts and actions. Studying and applying this material to my life gave me great comfort and support.

Ready for change, I desired spiritual support from other people. This intention did not materialize overnight, but it did progress faster than I could have imagined. For many years, I put out to the Universe that I wanted a partner with specific characteristics. This partner would be someone who shared my spiritual philosophy, as well as my explorative nature on many levels. I desired someone who was nurturing, mentally healthy, and fun. I also wanted someone who would honor and contribute to my growth and someone who valued respect.

In retrospect, I had hoped my wife would change and exhibit more of these qualities. I held onto this desire for almost fifteen years. Indeed, marriage contributed to my growth, but too much was negative and focused on survival. The overall environment during my family's early years needed to change, and I grieved this in many ways. I had to move on to create a healthier lifestyle for all of us. Change brought some difficult choices, with my decision to begin the divorce process being one of them. I believed that my children and I would be strengthened by a more positive environment.

Six months after I began divorce proceedings, I met a wonderful woman named Nita. Who would have guessed that later she would become someone very special in my life? I was on the Wellness Committee at the zoo and responsible for finding someone to facilitate a workshop on stress and meditation (certainly I needed a dose of this myself) for our week-long Wellness Fair.

I phoned Nita, whose name was given to me by a friend, and we chatted a bit. I was pleased to learn that she enjoyed reading many of the same books that I did. Both of us had just finished reading *The Seat of the Soul* by Gary Zukav, and really liked it (later we practiced its information about authentic relationships). Nita seemed to be on a similar wavelength, so I decided to share my personal written notes and spiritual materials with her.

Beginning in 1988, I compiled writings about my expanding spirituality and thoughts on wisdom. At that time, I intuitively shared my ideas, my Wisdom Packet, with people who seemed open or were actively searching for similar answers to questions about life at a higher level. Eventually, these materials became the catalyst for my book.

A week after I sent Nita my packet, I contacted her regarding more details about the Wellness Fair. I learned that she had read all of the material I had sent to her in one sitting—now, that meant a lot of reading. I was impressed because most people take longer to read my material, or they just scan it. I offered to send her a larger envelope of additional wisdom from other authors. I thought this would keep her busy for quite some time. Shortly after that, she told me she had read it all.

In exchange for sharing my writings with her, Nita thought I might enjoy some spiritual tapes from workshops she had attended. We decided to meet at a restaurant one night after I finished work. Reflecting on our evening of conversation, I gained amazing insight. Like many others, I believed that we live only once and then experience heaven forever. The last nine years contributed to a shift in my belief system that included reincarnation. Based on personal information that Nita shared that night, I am now convinced that reincarnation exists.

As Nita and I talked that evening, the energy between us grew stronger and stronger. I kept looking at our waitress to see if she saw sparks flying between Nita and me. Nita later said that she was startled when she saw in her mind's eye the infinity sign move between us. After two hours of talking, I felt as if I had known her for a very long time and could fully trust her. Since then, several psychics have told us that we have had many lifetimes together. This resonated with both of us.

The best way to describe reincarnation is that we live many lifetimes, simultaneously. These lifetimes can occur at the same time since there is only the eternal now or no time. Many scientists believe, that outside of physical reality, time is not linear as we believe it to be.

A metaphor of this is a person wearing different clothes each day of the week, where each day of the week represents a different lifetime. All of those clothes existed every day of that week. Yet it is only the clothes that we are wearing at the present time, or this lifetime, that we actually see and feel. We are able to go to our closet, look at our other clothes (lifetimes), and wear them (retrieve perspectives) if we choose. This is similar to having a past life regression. Some people seek this opportunity to discover answers to current problems. Sometimes we carry an experience from a past lifetime to our present one. Some examples include special talents, phobias, health issues, or relationship problems.

Here is another amazing similarity. Nita told me that at one time she had created and implemented a workshop titled, "Intimacy as a Spiritual Quest." She did not fully realize why she was driven to develop the workshop at that particular time. Later, she discovered that the timing of her workshop coincided exactly with the time when I ended my marriage.

She had never heard of me before nor knew anything about me. She was also planning to move to her home state of New Mexico. She began detaching and making many changes in her life as though preparing for something. She left her job, sold her home, sold or gave away most of her things, and dispatched her two children to college. She even legally changed her former married name to a new last name. She was set to move to the Southwest.

Without understanding why, Nita delayed leaving the Midwest. When we met and knew each other for about a month, these intuitive actions were clearer. We both considered this to be destiny. One has a choice in these matters, of course, but more and more events demonstrated a designed plan.

Committed to each other in love and spiritual partnership, we married after a couple of years when my divorce was final. I had custody of my three children, with my oldest entering college; Nita's daughter and son were already enrolled in different colleges. Since we each believed that time is eternal, we signed a spiritual covenant to be committed to each other throughout eternity. We stated we would support and help each other to grow as we continued to find our way Home to our Source.

In another lifetime, we know that this doesn't necessarily mean we will always be husband and wife. We may be siblings, friends, or in other roles. No matter what our relationship is in any given lifetime, we will love and support each other's growth. We came a long way together, so why not build upon that love and growth?

I believe that in this lifetime we have been able to grow much faster because we are together, rather than traveling alone or with a different person. How do we fully know this? It's a constant "knowing" and something that can't always be put into words. We discovered a commitment statement from an unknown source and liked it so well that we used it for our wedding ceremony.

"I promise to trust you enough to tell you the truth and to offer respect in my thoughts, words, and actions, whether in your presence or not. In every interaction I will surrender to love, our true nature. Being connected to my Source and my relationship with you will always be more important than any issue. If anything surfaces that is unlike love, I will hold us in my heart as each of us learns to speak, experience, and be responsible for our own realities. I will be there, for and with you, keep communication open and keep love conscious, active, and present as we grow."

Either of us can appeal to a copy of this statement and read it if we have disagreements or become uncomfortable about an interaction. It works for us. Most of all we trust, honor, and respect each other. Many life (and past life) experiences prior to meeting each other have forged the deepest commitment.

Together we've attended workshops, classes and a spiritual center that supported our expanding growth. For the most part, we have the same philosophy and are active in the same spiritual community. We do not believe that any one denomination or religion has all of the answers. Yet it is helpful to have a spiritual community to find other like-minded people for support and service. There are many places for spiritual renewal and support. All of us must search and find a spiritual journey based on what is needed for growth of the soul.

Discernment is crucial when interacting with any person or place that claims to have the only real Truth. It is important to look for a leader or a community where mutual wisdom and spiritual beliefs are honored and promoted. We need to think on a grander scale to understand that all of life has consciousness—from an individual cell to a planet. Each of us is a part of the wholeness of God. This concept was the fertile ground on which I based my *I Am* poems. I offer three of them here. Others can be found in Collection 3. By contemplating these poems, it is my hope that people will come to know consciousness through a different perspective, one of greater tolerance and acceptance.

A Checkout Countertop Am I

A checkout countertop am I.
A restricted consciousness have I.
Life for me is limited to sensing vibrations.
I do not think or analyze, just experience reverberations.

I exist in what you would call a stuporous state, but don't
be fooled by my state of mind.
As each hand or arm touches my counter surface, I pick
up vibrations of confusion, anger, loneliness,
annoyance, stress, and fear.
Who are these poor souls, called humans, that they
should abound in these lowly states of vibration?
I should pity their low lot in existence if it weren't for the
rare soul among them.
The rare, the few, give off this all-electrifying, humming
vibration.
This something is called love.

How I envy these souls called humans.
If only I had the opportunity to generate this thing called
love.
I would not waste my existence in lowly states of
vibration.
Alas, I am only a checkout countertop, and this
opportunity doesn't exist for me.
I do live for these rare moments though, when I can sense
this vibration called love.
It gives me life and purpose.
Oh, if only I was so fortunate to be as gifted as these
souls, called humans.

A checkout countertop am I.

March 10, 1990

Ink and Paper Are We

Ink and paper are we.
No two life forms have a greater symbiotic relationship.
By ourselves, we are nothing.
Together, we hold more power than thunder and wind,
the illusion of fear, or the thought prison that
humans have kept themselves in from generation to
generation.

It may appear that we are but inanimate materials.
Oh, just let us tell you of the power we possess.
When we are put together, we reveal the knowledge of
ages, the creativity of talented authors, and the
wisdom of mystics and spiritual masters.

If you only knew that we could set you free when the
right pattern of our combination comes together.
Seek us and let us reveal to you your true nature.
You are Divine, you are made of the same light and love
that God is, for the essence of God dwells within you.
We can help awaken you to your full potential and to all
of the powers you inherently possess.

As such, we also have a symbiotic relationship with you.
You have the power to create us, and we have the power
to reveal you to yourself.
Ink and paper are we.

April 20, 1996

A Butterfly Am I

A butterfly am I.
A creature of transformation and beauty am I.
I begin life as a vulnerable caterpillar.
Like you, while in this exposed state, I judge myself for
    not being fully loveable.
It is this judgmental mirroring in others through my
    outside world that keeps me as a caterpillar.
The only way to transform myself is to go within, by
    surrounding myself in a cocoon.

I go through a transformation that can reveal potential
    for metamorphosis to occur.
Within the cocoon, the secret to my transformation is my
    self love.
I am who I am.
There is nothing wrong with me, only with my thinking.
It is when I can truly start to love myself, knowing that
    the Source of all things is within me, that I can trans-
    mute and emerge as a butterfly.

As a butterfly, I am free, for I am Love in action.
I love myself while being a butterfly.
I enjoy all the parts, emotions, and movements that form
    me.
Think of your potential to be a butterfly.
By turning your attention toward self-love, you ignite the
    power of your love.
It is now that you can love others, as you love yourself.
That Divinity, which you are, is now moving at your
    command.

It has made me so happy that my life cycle has awakened
the Divinity within you.
We all are beautiful and loving butterflies.
A butterfly am I.

May 4, 1996

*O*ur intuition is our constant
connection to God/Source.

Chapter 5

Source

Often things do not happen in life the way that we plan them,
yet things usually work out for the best.

There was something familiar about the information. Why did I encounter an underlying feeling of déjà vu during a meditation that Nita and I experienced? She felt that I was communicating with the Great White Brotherhood. Not really knowing any details about this group, I contacted Theodore Baroody, Jr., who was knowledgeable in the subject and someone Nita had met at an earlier workshop. He suggested that I read two books: *The Ancient Mystical White Brotherhood* and *Melchizedek Truth Principles – From the Ancient Mystical White Brotherhood.* I located both Frater Achad books. As I read them, I became very emotional. It was like going Home, as if I already knew the material that was linking me to a memory deep within.

In *The Ancient Mystical White Brotherhood*, Frater Achad stated that members of the Order of Melchizedek are countless and invisible to humans. They are high-level spiritual beings from planets within the universe, including earth. Mortals would not be able to understand their advanced character, exclusive wisdom, and divine intelligence. They work together as One from the acclaimed supernatural planes of divine intelligence. Members of the Brotherhood know, understand and use all of the indisputable laws of life, love, and creation. Their assignment is to teach and enlighten earth leaders, seers, prophets, kings, presidents, educators, philosophers and others.

I pondered what I had read. Clearly, my intuition was storing this information, yet for what purpose, I did not know.

The next revealing step in this journey of discovery happened while I was driving my youngest daughter to Iowa for a visit with her mother. The latter stages of my divorce still lingered. It was a cloudy spring day, and I was listening to music on the radio while my daughter quietly drew on a note pad. My mind was not on anything in particular as I peacefully absorbed the music.

Catching me totally unaware, an inner voice said, "We of the Great White Brotherhood came to you in the 'Group Mind' experience you had a number of years ago."

I asked, "Who are you?"

"Andrew," came the reply.

"Andrew who?" I asked.

"You will know." Then after a long moment, the other names came: "Mark, Matthew, James, Paul, John, Bartholomew...."

At that moment, I realized the voice was naming the first Twelve Apostles of Jesus and Paul, the one originally called Saul. Stunned, I returned to the present moment, distinctly remembering each of the names. It was April of 1996, and I had finally received an answer about the identity of the souls who merged with me during my group mind experience of Oneness, eight years earlier.

Could I accept my experience as Truth? As soon as I returned home, I excitedly called Nita and said that I wanted to share a very interesting conversation from my trip. Nita had been renting a basement apartment from her good friend, Nancy. As I approached the front door, both Nita and Nancy were there to greet me. Possessing some psychic abilities, Nancy spontaneously said, "I was given a message to tell you that whatever it was you recently experienced was real; you weren't just making it up." Nancy knew nothing about what the voice had told me, and I had not, as of yet, shared my experience. I took a deep breath and proceeded to share my story with the two of them.

After thinking more about what I was told, I began to wonder, who am I that the apostles would come to me in this way? Why had they merged their consciousness with me years ago? Soon after came another confirmation from a trusted psychic who said that I was Bartholomew. I had not expected to hear this, so I had lots of questions. Did this mean I was part of a group of souls who had origin in Jesus' apostle, Bartholomew? Was I the reincarnation of Bartholomew? My head was spinning. It was too much for me to grasp, even as a very open-minded person. I decided to put the incident in the back of my mind and let it rest.

The only thing that seemed to hold any confirmation for me was an experience I had during a meditation earlier that year. Nita took me into a meditative state, or past life regression, by going back to the time when Jesus walked the earth. In that meditation, I came face to face with Jesus, and he really seemed like a brother to me. I merged with Jesus to fully exchange strong feelings of love. It felt as though his heart and my heart were One.

Over the next several years there would be eight or nine other people who would tell me that I was either Bartholomew or was being "overshadowed" by Bartholomew. Some of these people were unaware of the other's information. Usually, when I hear similar information presented three times or more, I pay more attention to it. However, this information was too overwhelming. I chose not to embrace my experiences and simply lived my day-to-day life as if nothing had happened.

Growth and change shape our lives, and I kept striving for spiritual expansion. I entered another time in my life when I would write inspirational thoughts in a journal. From 1995 through 2000, I wrote messages that came from my high self, or Spirit: Words that moved me and felt true. Many of the writings represented how I viewed events in my life. Most of these writings were personal; however, I have chosen to share some of them. Included here is one of my spiritual writings entitled, "The Deepest Level of Communication is Communion." Additional spiritual prose is included in Collection 4, *As the Eagle Soars*.

The Deepest Level of Communication is Communion

How do we communicate that which cannot be expressed in words or through body language? What I am expressing is a form of communication from the deepest levels within me. It is a form of communication that has been in existence since the beginning of time. Pierre-François de Bethune stated it this way:

"The deepest level of communication is not communication, but communion. It is wordless. It is beyond words, and it is beyond speech, and it is beyond concept. Not that we discover a new unity. We discover an older unity. But we imagine that we are not. And what we have to recover is our original unity. What we have to be is what we are."

It is at this level of communication that we can be in communion with all forms of life. When we find our Oneness with all of life, we can better communicate and understand each other. This can bring deeper meaning to life.

We are entering a new age where this form of communication may take on more importance than even the written or verbal word. The past, where we possibly felt alone or abandoned, is leaving us. We are finding connections with each other and with all that is.

How do we communicate with a tree or with a flower? My answer is that we *feel* a connection with it. We join our energy field with its energy field, using the glue that binds all things—love. Then, with that intuitive knowing that connects us to all things, we join in communion. If we can practice this with trees, think of the world we could create when we have this level of communion with people we meet in our lives. Whether we are aware of it or not, what each of us is seeking is our connection with the Creator of all life, that which is within us. We need to awaken. We have never truly been separated. Separation is an illusion.

My good friend, Tom, expressed this deeper form of communion in a candid letter to me. He stated:

"I see the love we have for each other. A friendship does not last this long, at the depth and intimacy we have, without a deep love. The last time I 'saw' this love was during those dances of Universal Peace at your Life Partnership ceremony with Nita. You and I looked into each other's eyes and a lot of emotion gently flowed between us. I knew that you knew it was happening, and I did not need to say a word about it. You knew that I knew, and I knew that you knew. If these things need to be measured, I guess this single experience is as good a meter stick as any."

As I experience this level of communion with more and more people, my life becomes richer. I start to see the unity and Oneness of us all. Writing this allows me to feel and experience this communion with my spiritual guides and readers. We must remember that time and space are relative. We experience this in the eternal now, outside of time and space. I am allowing myself to be vulnerable and share my deepest self with all. I want readers to feel this connection and join in communion with me. We are all One. "What we have to be is what we are."

January 17, 1999

I want to share some background with you about *As the Eagle Soars*. My wife, Nita, has some Native American ancestry, and we both share a strong interest in Native American spirituality. Through this common interest, I discovered that my power animal is the Golden Eagle, and carried that name into my spiritual writings.

Nita studied Shamanism for a year, and eventually offered classes on Native American wisdom. She learned how to facilitate Shamanic journeys, and sometimes I took these journeys with her. My love of nature seemed to fit with this aspect of Native American spirituality. We both learned a great deal from Shamanic journeys.

I find that all forms of spirituality have something to offer. Still, no single religion has all of the answers or all of the universal truths. I believe we are each drawn to a religion, or form of spirituality, that speaks closest to our present state of awareness, whatever level that may be. There is no right or wrong to this. People need to follow their hearts and intuition to gather what is needed. This, in turn, may progress into something else. This process is more fluid than rigid. Although rituals and traditions bring comfort and serve many people, we still must realize personal growth through trust. Without it, we become habitual and lose our sense of purpose.

To feel is to live.

Chapter 6

Earth's Riches

We trust that all growth is divine order.

Life went on. Life was good. All of our children grew up, left home, and many married and became parents. Nita and I continued our journey together in all of the usual ways. We were very active in a Unity spiritual center, continued to make new friends, and found many ways to be of service. We continued to work full time in our professions as educator and zookeeper.

Our love for the beauty of nature inspired us to hire someone to dig a half-acre pond on our ten-acre property. I stocked it with fish and planted trees, wildflowers, prairie grasses, and shrubs to create a natural wildlife haven on our land. This kept us busy in the physical world, along with our many gardens. We have been grateful for all of the seasons of Nurturing Acres gardening and sharing. The following writing describes the many earth lessons provided by this activity. Other writings are part of Collection 4, *As the Eagle Soars*.

Our Garden

Have you ever thought about the full spectrum of the gardening cycle that is taking place whenever you receive some of our Nurturing Acres produce? This spectrum actually begins in the winter while the soil lies barren and frozen under a blanket of snow. These first stirrings occur when I send nurturing thoughts to the garden. In anticipation, the earth receives the seeds of hope for spring. With the spring thaw, natural organic fertilizer starts to penetrate its nutrients deep within the soil. Hay from the surrounding pasture serves as mulch around the perennial plants, offering protection from the drying winds. Earthworms do their part as they continue to turn over the earth that is underneath the hay. Weeds give up their struggle so that the desired plants may take advantage of the additional space and nutrients.

Spring brings warming temperatures and life-giving rains. Tilling the soil brings the microorganisms back to the surface, and the organic fertilizer is broken up and redistributed. This brings air back into the soil. This time of year makes me feel rejuvenated, and I reconnect with the earth.

Each seed I plant is poised to carry out its genetic instructions and to grow into the plant it was created to be. The plant's life forces go into action as they work in harmony with all that is around them. The environment gives spirit to the growing seeds and plants so that they might develop their own energies. I feel at peace and in harmony when working in the garden. The plant consciousness or elemental devas pervades the surrounding garden as we work as one to create expressions of love.

It is truly a joint effort in the manifestation of creation. Forty-year-old spruce offer protection to the garden from the prevailing south summer winds. They also offer shelter for all of the songbirds that grace our home and garden. Birds share their daily songs with growing plants, enabling the plant stomas to open wider so they can absorb more nutrients. This symbiotic relationship results in larger, healthier plants.

With intentional exchange, we share our garden with the wildlife. I even have an agreement with the local rabbit population. I have built brush piles around the garden and yard as protection from our dogs, other natural predators, and the weather. In return, they eat minimally from our garden, concentrating instead on the area's native vegetation.

As the bird life partakes of our berries, garden spiders spin their webs in our raspberry canes, helping to control the garden's insect populations. Native bees and pollen-loving insects of the area visit the flowering plants, providing cross-pollination.

As the summer unfolds, other native animals like pheasants, Red fox, raccoons, and opossums visit the garden. Underground, even the Eastern mole is busy turning the soil. This interaction continues throughout the summer. There is continuous interplay among the species of the local plant kingdom with the strongest plants seizing available garden space at any given time.

After long hours of tilling, hoeing, and weeding, the desired plants flourish and take command of the developing garden. Vine crops such as pumpkins, squash, and melons minimize the weed population. Many garden plants work as companion crops. Certain plants can be grown side-by-side to help each other enhance growth and deter insects.

The light-giving rays of the summer sun produce an energy exchange that is needed for plant growth and development. When all of life works in harmony, the outcome is an abundant harvest. Varying life cycles for different plants provides an on-going harvest, beginning with asparagus near the end of April. The harvest continues until late September and early October with the final gathering of pumpkins and winter squash.

Our 10,000 square foot garden produces approximately fifty varieties of fruits and vegetables, yielding over 4,000 pounds of produce annually. We share our harvest with family, friends, and co-workers. Some extra produce is shared with the chickens and other native animals of the area. Any remaining yield is returned to the earth to recycle nutrients for another year.

The garden produces abundantly and expresses life energy by the texture, size, and flavor of its fruits and vegetables. We experience great personal joy from working in and observing our garden and also from sharing our harvest. We believe it is a labor of love.

September 24, 2000

Viewing the nearly 200 young trees that I have planted throughout our property reminded me of our intention to raise the vibrations of our ten acres. We envisioned all plants and life forms thriving and interacting with each other. These life forms, including our gardens and animals, give our land a distinct energy of its own. A former dairy farm, Nurturing Acres features a 135-year-old, remodeled house and existing barn.

Many pastures and fields surround the agricultural preservation area in which we live. Because of this setting, wooded areas and a pond were needed to attract wildlife. This landscape provides a place to connect with other kingdoms that share our world and beyond. Even the fresh, organic garden vegetables and berries are blessed with the intention of adding positive energy and a higher vibration when consumed. People have commented that they can taste the difference.

To intentionally add to the energy field of our property, Nita has facilitated Medicine Wheel, Four Directions, and Drumming Circle ceremonies. In addition to these gatherings, we also host Women's Lodges, the BE Group, and the Spiritual Transformation Group. We are appreciative of the rich, added energy of our many visitors.

We constructed a Peace Pole and established a Peace Garden, complete with a meditation bench that honors the memories of our mothers. We placed quartz crystals in and around our pond and at the boundaries of our land. Bernard, our friend who is a psychic seer, also envisioned an energy portal in one of the evergreen areas. Next, we would love to create a labyrinth or meditative path and even have a Crop Circle appear. Why not?

*O*ur perfection, our love shared, is our eternal Truth.

Chapter 7

Messages of Wisdom

Purpose of life: To seek complete Oneness with God, my creator, through recollection, growth, and high-level learning, offering love and service to others whenever possible.

Our capacity to grow and learn is often affected by death— which is not really an end, but a beginning. Within a three-year span, our parents passed on to the Other Side. With each passing, I recollected my First Communion shared with the loved one who had died. My deceased, loving grandfather, to whom I felt especially close, came to me twenty-five years after his passing.

At first I just had strong feelings and emotions as I recognized my grandfather was communicating with me. I began to recognize him as I felt his unique vibration, becoming aware of his "internal words" of guidance, encouragement, and support. I have had occasional connections with him over the past ten years.

Nita and I have experienced great comfort by being open and communicating with additional loved ones from the Other Side. Nita felt emotional, yet comforted when her mom, Barbara, communicated with us—especially right after her death. She had always been very interested in the spiritual knowledge we were gaining, the groups in our lives, and all we were doing to our property. Nita even made the comment, "I'm learning to live with my mother again." This was very affirming that contact with the Other Side was possible.

Because of failing health, Barbara never had the opportunity during this lifetime to visit and participate in any of our interests and activities. She indicated to Nita that she was very happy and thrilled to be rid of her frail body and mind and to be of greater service on the Other Side. Another psychic seer in one of our groups even observed her dancing with joy in the middle of the room where we were meeting.

Since I knew Nita's mom only during the later years of her life, I actually came to know her more intimately after her death. Communicating in this way allowed us to continue our connection with our loved ones, even after they passed from our physical reality. The world for Nita and me was truly becoming multidimensional.

By 2003, I embraced my connection to Bartholomew and the apostles. Classes on different healing and manifestation modalities helped me to embrace their earlier communication. I connected with one of the people we knew from the class series who guided me through some extensive past life regression sessions. Upon completing approximately three recall sessions, the resulting information started another period of intense growth for me.

Certainly the most convincing confirmation about the recalls was the emotions that came with the communication. I asked to be taken back to the time when Jesus walked the earth. Right away I saw myself working in some fields. Vividly recalling this session, I saw Jesus walking on a road between two villages and heard him call a seagull. I saw the seagull immediately fly to his arm. Intrigued, I walked over to him to ask how he attracted the seagull. Jesus replied, *With pure love.*

Something about this occurrence resonated so deeply that I left my work immediately to follow Him. I might add that every time I recall this vision, I become very, very emotional. Usually I do not show my emotions, so this experience stands out. Even now, as I write about this experience, emotions overcome me. I've pondered why these emotions are so powerful and believe that I really felt them in an earlier lifetime. My soul has had many opportunities for growth and expanded awareness.

Another recollection of this lifetime occurred when Jesus, the apostle Andrew, and I were leading a donkey-drawn cart, full of branches for firewood. We stopped to take a drink of water at a well located in a grove of olive trees. I also recalled that Andrew was my best friend. Today, whenever I think about Jesus or Andrew, emotions strongly vibrate through me, and thoughts of olive trees evoke special enjoyment.

Another scene I recalled was the time when the other apostles and I visited the home of Mother Mary and Jesus. Mary asked me questions about the care of some of her flowering plants since I was a gardener by profession. I recalled that it was a carefree, comfortable day when we shared stories, relaxed together, and enjoyed the moment. I truly felt part of this group, and I still do. I searched the New American Bible: St. Joseph Edition to see if there were any stories of these past life experiences. I found no information.

Bartholomew's death in that lifetime brought deep sorrow to my memory. I saw his legs being broken with a mallet, and then his body crucified. Now, as I recall this scene, I still feel intense pain, as though it were happening to me all over again. I don't choose to recall the experience often for obvious reasons; however, this powerful recollection convinced me that there was more than a casual connection to Bartholomew: *It is very possible that we shared the same identity.*

I thought about what to do with this information and decided that I just couldn't continue to deny or ignore my experiences any longer. Recently, I came to a point in my awakening where it really didn't matter if Bartholomew and I were one in the same, if Bartholomew was overshadowing me, or if I was tapping into the collective unconscious when I experienced his memories. What mattered was what I learned from the encounters. It was confirming to me that we are One. We are all on a journey of reawakening to who we truly are at a soul level. Spurred by this affirmation, I was motivated to organize the BE Group.

In 2004, the BE Group began with six people. BE stands for Bartholomew Effect. Nita developed another tagline to define the group's purpose: BE all that you can be. Initially, it wasn't easy to explain my connection to Bartholomew. I first shared the Bartholomew story with a few people and then continued to share it with several people who were close to me. It was somewhat difficult to reveal my new understanding, as it was such an astounding, personal revelation. It was not something to be taken lightly. Some people might think that I was on an ego trip, delusional, or that I had a very colorful imagination.

Most people know that I'm a scientist, as well as a spiritual and philosophical person. Many scientists do not believe in something unless it can be proven scientifically. Most of my experiences, of course, cannot be confirmed.

I simply can't prove them. Still, I cannot ignore the strong, confirming feelings that these encounters really happened. In many ways we are being told to trust our intuition. I have decided to do that and move forward by sharing my experiences with you.

The BE Group is flourishing. We meet twice a month in our home to share our journeys of spiritual awakening and growth. We respect and support each other as we awaken individually and in our own time to the Oneness of who we are at our soul's level. It is a place where we can allow ourselves to be vulnerable without being ridiculed or disrespected. We gather to learn from each other and to help in the healing and transforming of our earth, the Gaia, and of all humanity. The BE Group is very important to us as our purpose continues to go forward.

In 2004 I also started to receive internal messages from a number of sources. Some people may call this channeling, yet I prefer to call it receiving internal messages of wisdom. Whenever individuals "download" messages from their high selves, or the higher realms, they filter the material through their minds and personalities; therefore, some distortions may occur. I believe we all have the ability to receive internal messages, if we are willing to be open to them. I always advise people to use careful discernment when distinguishing what is true and what may be perceived as a distortion.

My internal messages of wisdom are phrased for readers to easily understand their meaning, rather than verbatim from the soul. Nevertheless, the words do not change the feelings of truth and accompanying emotions. What helps me to believe these messages is my acceptance that I can rely on the intuitive knowingness of the words *and* the strong affirmative feelings that accompany the words. Together, the words and feelings convince me of the truth of the message.

Another confirmation that these words came from my high self is their meaning. I would be too self-conscious to say those descriptions and directives, yet the concepts were there. In short, trust what your intuition tells you about the truth of any internal messages of wisdom.

A number of these messages are found in Collection 5 of the book. In the following message that I received from Jesus in early July 2005, the word "you" refers to Larry. Jesus' messages always ended with three emotional statements:

This is the 'Love of the Heart.'
This is the 'Love of the Heart.'
This is the 'Love of the Heart.'

These were very powerful words.

Spiritual Message from Jesus the Christ to Larry

Larry: "It is back to the time when Jesus walked the earth and I was Bartholomew. I can look into Jesus' eyes and merge my heart with his." (Silence)

Jesus: It is I, Jesus the Christ, who comes to you this day. All days are this day. There is only now. Since there is only now, I am always connected to you. We are always together. I am you. You are me. It is as it should be in the Higher Realms. This is where everyone lives, as a greater, larger self. Only a small part of you is on the earth at any given time. There is no disruption in the communication. It is all about flow, motion, and energy. There is no gap in time, communication and the work that you do through all time.

You live in the higher worlds — more of your focus is there. You are preparing yourself for a much greater role that does not occur in this lifetime. It is all about Oneness. Oneness has greater meaning than is known. You are only conscious of this to a certain level, yet you grasp what is needed for the work that must be done. This work is very emotionally charged within you, for you carry the energy needed for this work. It is important for you to follow your intuition and activate the things you are called upon to do, regardless of whether others understand your work or not.

What you are preparing to do does not include the earth, or affect others, unless they are a part of the greater mission. Yes, there are some with you who are a part of the greater mission. They will know who they are and will play their roles. All worlds reside within each other. This earth is but a training ground for many different missions that overlap or are unrelated.

Your back is a metaphor for gaining strength and having the backbone to carry out a mission of great magnitude. You know of what I speak because this mission has come forward in consciousness within the past week.

Oneness has many levels. You know about other souls merging with your soul. That merger offers greater freedom rather than restrictions. In the merger, there is still focus on one consciousness. Greater energy and magnitude are present at a higher vibration. This vibration creates a different world and reality that is unlike what is experienced as individual souls [on earth].

The ascension process that earth and the inhabitants are going through is in preparation for greater realities and creations in the times ahead. It is not the end; it is the beginning. In preparation, you have been called to come forward to take on new efforts different from those tried in the past. You will be guided to go forward in necessary ways, as the timing is right. For you to go forward, you need to be fearless and committed. That you are. You are supported by the Higher Kingdoms. Your progress is closely watched by all involved. Many souls play various roles in this endeavor. Much is changing in your world on many levels.

At this time, Nita is changing and is being called into higher service in a way that she does not fully understand. She will be reaching people in ways that enable them to see their God selves, while simultaneously connecting with other souls and the Divine. Her efforts will be the glue that cements broader activity. Most people are not consciously aware of their greater work on this earth plane. Their higher selves will know and nudge their inner guidance.

Until you release the old, or that which is not needed, the new cannot fully come forward. Release, release in joy and with hope—hope for the future and for a more creative world of peace, love, and Oneness. The New World will be a training ground for new realities and broader creations. It cannot happen in this old world.

At this moment, let there be silence to feel my energy. (Silence) *Know there is only Oneness. It always has been this way. All is well.*

This is the 'Love of the Heart.'
This is the 'Love of the Heart.'
This is the 'Love of the Heart.'

July 3, 2005

To live life without masks is one of the
most freeing things we can do.

Chapter 8

The Bartholomew Effect

We are One with all that is. In a state of being, of pure uncondi-tional 'love of the heart,' this statement is self-actualized.

At the time, I could not have known the direction I would take some five years later. The summer of 2004 provided another experience that profoundly affected me. One day I was scheduled for a Reiki healing touch session facilitated by Louise, a good friend. Lying comfortably on the massage table in a relaxed, meditative state, I suddenly felt a powerful jolt go through my body. At the same time, a message filled my whole being: *Your first book will be called* The Bartholomew Effect. This experience was similar to the one in which I received my life mission information many years earlier.

The idea of writing a book had been on my mind, yet I hadn't felt an urgency to pursue that path. I was content with handing out packets of my writings to interested individuals. Something changed, however, toward the end of 2008. It seemed as if I were being nudged by Spirit to advance my work, so I became serious about turning my packets into a book. I asked Spirit if I should still use the words The Bartholomew Effect as part of the title. The answer came back in the affirmative, and I began to compile *The Bartholomew Effect: Awakening to Oneness.*

I am reminded of Oneness each time I hear or see the phrase, "This is the 'Love of the Heart.'" I sense Oneness with Jesus and all other life forms. When we are young, our "job" is to be a student. After we begin acquiring certain skills and knowledge, we graduate and are expected to go out into the world and become productive. So it is in our spiritual lives.

I have been acquiring spiritual growth through life lessons, by reading hundreds of books and attending classes, and by reflecting on a multitude of experiences. In recent years, my focus has been living what I have learned and applying life's lessons as a mentor. Having moved beyond self-help strategies and continuously trying to fix myself and others, I now realize that I am unbroken. I have inside all that I need to be productive and can be of service to others.

We are living in a very special time in human history. It's a fast-paced and changing world where humanity is positioned to take a giant leap in evolution. With focused intention, we can create a new and better world. Some say we are moving out of a third-dimensional world into fourth- and fifth-dimensional worlds.

What does this mean for us? Mainly it means that we are moving to a world of peace and love and inter-connectedness. It means that we will come to know and understand our connection with all of life. We will begin to create and live for the good of the whole, becoming mul-tidimensional humans. Our lives will continue to expand as we awaken to a greater knowledge of the true nature of who we are and to our connection of a greater reality.

To create a new and better world, we first have to imagine what that world would look like. Although we live at a time when we can create heaven on earth, not much is said about how we should accomplish it. To many, this sounds like an overwhelming expectation.

Many sources state that what we focus on, we draw to ourselves. Another way to phrase this concept is that on which we focus, expands. I am among a growing number of people who have had life-altering experiences within higher dimensions of reality. With each multidimensional experience, it is impossible to return to a former conscious-ness as an unaltered person. Awareness has increased. This newfound awareness prompts us to search for Home in a new reality.

Right now I believe we have the opportunity to create higher realms of energy right here on earth. With this in mind, I want to share my vision of what this Nirvana might look like. In 2006 and 2007, I wrote the WHAT IF... Series to demonstrate how we might begin to create heaven on earth. It is my humble contribution to the whole. These writings offer a new reality, the idea of a higher state of being where there is only Oneness.

After contemplating some of these revelations, dear reader, I hope that you will take the opportunity to expand your visions and desires to create a best life on earth. Since we are creating this new world together, we share the gratifying task of being conscious co-creators. Your spark of the divine is waiting to be activated.

Let's begin with WHAT IF... All hearts were open? Other writings from the WHAT IF... Series are found in Collection 6.

WHAT IF...

All hearts were open?

What if all hearts were open to the hearts of other individuals? We would truly see each other for who we are: All are One. There would be only one of us here, for we would be seeing our reflection in each heart that is open.

When we remove all of the masks and illusions, which symbolize a closed heart, the only thing that remains is our Truth. The Truth is the love that we are. This love is the same within each heart. Love is not an idea, but a feeling that knows no borders. A feeling of love merges with everything. Truly, love from an open heart sees itself in the object of its focus. Love cannot be divided. It can only expand. This is what creation is all about—that expansion of love. Heaven is love. Earth is a projection of that love in an outward expansion of the same.

In an open heart, all efforts are in the expansion of that which it is, love. Just think of what life will be like when all hearts are open? It takes so much energy to keep a heart closed. A closed heart portrays us as what we are not. We work hard to maintain the illusion that we are separate from others: that we are different from others and have the attitude of being better than others. This feeling attempts to fool us, masking our insecurities of self-worth.

Another way we project separateness is through unworthiness because of perceptions that we are unable to measure up to others' expectations. In truth, we are Divine. We are an expression of that love, which is God/Source. To be our authentic selves takes no effort. It is a state of being. It is a state of joy, happiness, and love. It is a state of knowing that we are a reflection of another—nothing more, nothing less.

We have awareness when we expand ourselves to assist others to also see who they are. In this act of assistance, we love ourselves by our own expansion. We enter into a state of Oneness with this awareness, a state where every action is an action of love for the good of the whole. This is called "awakening." It is also known as "ascension," where the whole wakes up to a higher state of consciousness. For this to happen, our souls need to experience a heart opening. When this begins to happen, all human masks and illusions begin to fall away. Truly, these masks never did exist. The Truth is then revealed, as our magnificence is revealed. We are One with all.

November 6, 2006

There are a number of ways to contribute to the whole without feeling as if we have to reinvent the wheel. We can piggyback on others' wisdom and service to humanity. Today's communication opportunities and technologies can bring instant connections. Wisdom and knowledge writers have pooled lifetimes of intellectual property and then passed it on to us. Other readers and writers appear, take that knowledge and combine it with theirs, and expand the resources of wisdom. It's all about passing it on and ascending the ladder with each new wave of authors.

Maybe we can climb this ladder together.

As mentioned in Chapter 3, we can share wisdom by completing the Wisdom Questionnaire in Collection 1 of the book. I also invite you to locate the questionnaire at my website, www.awakeningtooneness.com or contact me at Larry Vorwerk, P. O. Box 401, Northfield, MN 55057. I welcome all input.

There is another way of communicating with each other. Since we are all connected, why not offer our high self wisdom and knowledge to others? I would like to experiment with this concept.

With love and openness, I open my high self wisdom to be tapped telepathically. This style of communication could be much more efficient than sharing a book list or setting up a computer blog. With only good intentions practiced, it might be possible for each of us to have some real soulful communication. When souls communicate like this, they could easily have the insights needed for increased growth.

Learning from others' mistakes and experiences, rather than experiencing a similar situation, would be much more to my liking. This certainly goes beyond walking in someone else's shoes. Each of us has unique wisdom. Let's consider sharing it and taking some soul journeys together.

I recently thought of another idea that I hope will

help transform our world. I started to visualize all of the people I know as literally being One at a higher soul level. I imagined and felt the divinity that we truly are in this higher state of being. Next I sent out an "intentional thought package" of timeless, warm, fuzzy, supportive feelings of love and Oneness to all people. Most of the visualizations I sent to other individuals traveled on a one-way street. Not receiving any response messages, I continued to believe: What I focus on, I attract. Guess what? Several months ago, at random times throughout the day, I started to receive some reply "internal thought packages."

Now, imagine humanity receiving these over-powering feelings of Oneness, love and connectedness throughout the day. It wouldn't take long before people would begin treating each other, and all living things, with love and respect. They might even conduct their lives with new, intentional purpose for the good of the whole. They would no longer feel unworthy or judged.

Let's start this new way of living, and together, play this game of life. All right. Wouldn't a world that is cooperative and noncompetitive be an exceptional place to be? We can all be winners. The Bartholomew Effect is a reflection of Oneness, supported by my experiences with Jesus and Bartholomew. More directly, it is the experience I had as Bartholomew, feeling the exchange of uncondi-tional love of the heart, in Oneness, with Jesus or Christ

Consciousness. In Oneness, all separation disappears. I resonated with Jesus and continue to do so. If people truly feel the unconditional love of Christ Consciousness as I do, then they would *choose* to merge into Oneness.

In order to achieve this state of Oneness, we need to be a part of a higher vibration by transcending negative, angry, judgmental, and small-minded feelings. Lives can be transformed with new perceptions and consciousness. There is no magic wand.

Attaining higher consciousness is decidedly personal. We can have moments of enlightenment through The Bartholomew Effect as I have, or experience this higher consciousness through other means. It is certain, however, that we will have unique experiences in our journey. No matter what, the outcome remains the same. We are all moving toward Oneness.

It is up to us to choose a spiritual leader of good intention; the name does not really matter. The vibration of unconditional *Love of the Heart* is the same within all enlightened beings. The greatest stumbling block is that we have been programmed by society and many traditional religions to believe that we can never measure up to Jesus or other enlightened souls.

This is an illusion that is difficult to overcome, especially for individuals who were raised to feel a bit unworthy by some religions. While in human form, we see our human frailties with narrow vision. My thinking goes beyond these perceived limitations.

As we awaken to our multidimensional selves, change is inevitable. Since we are all One in our true essence, the main difference between enlightened beings and those not yet enlightened is the lack of awareness and focused consciousness. It's time to wake up!

The more I bond with Jesus or Christ Energy, the more I feel pure, unconditional love. This makes it easier to remain connected. I don't have to go through any deliberate effort. The Christ Energy simply stays with me.

An example is when I communicated with my dad on the Other Side. At first I connected with him as a separate entity. Then, less than a year ago, this changed, and I now feel Oneness with Dad whenever we connect. Our communication is more personal, and nothing is lost in translation.

This Oneness can also happen with other individuals or with groups of people. When a group focuses on a single intention of higher vibration, merging of consciousness can happen. For example, this sometimes occurs when I'm attending a Unity spiritual center service. As the minister speaks, I notice how much everyone around me is focused on the words. By tuning into the harmonizing group energy, it is possible for me to energetically merge with all in attendance. A high energy of love enveloping the group acts as a magnet, bringing everyone into the same frequency of Oneness. This feeling is so exhilarating.

Many things are possible if we are courageous enough to explore areas beyond our comfort zones. Sometimes we may experience a nagging, intuitive feeling to fulfill some mission or purpose in this lifetime. This is often the case reported by several of our friends.

For me, the intuitive feeling is to share my experiences of The Bartholomew Effect and the impact it has had on my life. I have experienced a deeper Christ Consciousness that has changed me, how I interact with people, and my approach to every situation. As a result, I believe that we are to step out into the light of our being to help make the changes in the world that we wish to see. By doing this, we also align with the Creator's master plan to "Love One Another." It is my hope that we will seek and engage in personal ways to experience Oneness with all life forms.

So now when I look into another's eyes, I see and feel that same energy of love that I feel as I connect with the Christ Consciousness of Jesus. This pure love of the heart is one and the same. Because we are truly One, we carry this energy within us. It is my hope that when we meet, we can fully acknowledge each other with love and realize love of the heart.

As taught to me by Jesus, the first focus is love for

my being. The second focus is love for another, acknowledged person. The third focus is love for the synergy created by each person's high self, leading to the Oneness of all that is.

This is the 'Love of the Heart.'
This is the 'Love of the Heart.'
This is the 'Love of the Heart.'

.

The world's wisest, most benevolent
souls come into our lives.

Chapter 9

Soulful Living

I like to plant thought seeds in other people's minds, letting them germinate and grow. My intention is that those thoughts will flower and bloom.

In many ways, I see myself as a spiritual Johnny Apple Seed. Just as the legend of Johnny Apple Seed tells of his journey to plant apple seeds everywhere, envisioning apple trees flourishing one day, it is my desire to plant seeds of insight. I don't wait to see if those seeds have the right soil for germination. Seldom do I see what growth occurs. It is the seed planting that is most important. This book contains different thought seeds that I hope will find "gardeners" who are inspired to cultivate their own orchards or gardens. All cultivation techniques are encouraged.

At this point in my journey, I want to share additional insights and guidelines for soulful living. There are universes within universes. Our human forms exist in one of many universes—not the smallest one, nor the largest—just somewhere within multiple universes. Similarly, when we look into an electron microscope, an entire living world is present within an area too small to be seen with the naked eye. Yet, at the subatomic level, there are worlds within that world.

On a larger perspective, we are like individual cells in a body. There are blood cells flowing through the capillaries at the tips of our fingers that are totally unaware of the cells in our minds that may be enjoying music at a party. As a blood cell, we would be conscious only of immediate surroundings such as the capillary lining and fluids.

When we "wake up," or ascend, we move from self-consciousness to super consciousness. The more we awaken, the more expansive our awareness becomes. This awareness is the magnificence and totality of who we really are. It seems likely that we would not willfully choose to return to any restrictive view of reality. We would ascend to the next stage of consciousness, ready for evolutionary growth.

What if the Creator's plan for all life forms on our planet were really about the ascension of earth as a living body called Gaia? All of us are the sum total of the parts of the whole. I offer the thought that when we connect our Oneness with Gaia, we expand our understanding of reality. When we are able to go even further and feel connected with the universe, and all that is, we exponentially increase this awareness.

I believe the human race is at this stage right now — growing and expanding. What an exciting time to be alive on this planet! What a ride this can be. It's like riding a roller coaster. Momentarily, the ride itself is all consuming and even scary. Yet once the ride is over, it is easy to look back and say, "Wasn't that fun? Let's do it again." or continue to search for new, more challenging rides.

People have raised questions. What if we were all part of the totality of a Creator who gains understanding through us as sparks of Divinity? Is God living vicariously through us while we play a game of amnesia to find our way back to the God self? Let me speculate. What if God did create the illusion of time to play this game? We are learning that linear, earth time might not really exist except through perception. There's the possibility that the past, present, and future exist at the same time in other realms. I've read that nonlinear time is constantly changing as well. Since we have free will, we can influence this change and exercise the possibility of being a co-creator within our day-to-day lives, as well as within our past and future lives.

What if life and all time were part of an eternal continuum, helping us to remain serene? As the saying goes, "Don't sweat the small stuff; it's all small stuff." If the only real time is now, then it would be easier to explain premonitions and déjà vu. The reason some of us experience premonitions of future events, and others do not, might be explained with some understanding of the Quantum Theory of modern physics.

When we have a premonition of something that we perceive will happen in the future, what we might be seeing (or linking to) is the "future of today." Since there are infinite numbers of possibilities for that potential future, what is actually determined right now is our concept of future. It will depend on our thoughts and actions. Today's thoughts may or may not become the "future of tomorrow," depending on how free will is exercised and who is involved.

We face multiple issues of global warming, economics, habitat destruction, poverty, hunger and more. Just as our own physical body has exponentially greater abilities than the sum of its individual parts, humanity can overcome problems and challenges by living from a higher level of inner-connectedness. We are faced with two choices: Will we answer the call to deal with these issues, gathering as a global family? or Will we ignore the call, separately wearing blinders or rose-tinted glasses? I believe our moral responsibility, as well as our spiritual evolution, depends on how we choose to answer the call.

For just a moment, let's consider that something appearing separate from us really isn't separate. Again, using the analogy of the human body, let us say we live in a two-dimensional world as "flat land people." In this world, when we look at our fingers passing through an imaginary two-dimensional, single sheet of tissue paper, each finger and thumb appear to be separate units. As we move beyond our current reality, we have the ability to view our fingers and thumb differently. We see that they are connected as parts of a whole—operating in one body. Even the head and feet, along with other parts of the body, are more connected than they appear or than our awareness allows.

Extending this idea, it is possible to see that we are connected to each other and to all life forms in an intimate way. Each part of the body works together for the good of the whole person. In this same manner, we humans *could choose* to work together for the good of the whole of humanity and the world. We don't see our two feet opposing each other by walking in two different directions, so why do we need to be competitive or oppositional with each other? Why not awaken to a higher consciousness and live together as we truly are—One? Believing in this connection is an important awareness for spiritual maturity.

As I mentioned, we must overcome a number of things before a true feeling of Oneness naturally fills our day-to-day experiences. We need to rise above all of those thoughts that tell us we are separate. When we see all of life as an extension of ourselves, then the ego will fade into the background. The ego thrives on the illusion of separateness that could appear as feelings of envy, jealousy, resentment, and judgment. Making a conscious shift not to allow our egos to control us is an important step toward enlightenment.

Many of us who acknowledge various possibilities are called seekers. We are open to seeking answers from a variety of sources and receiving knowledge from many experiences. We are not part of a seeker religion of additional tenets or a cult. Open-mindedness is the password to join us.

Nita and I invited a small group of seekers to our home to study Eckhart Tolle's second book, *A New Earth—Awakening to Your Life's Purpose.* Over twelve weeks, we listened and discussed the book via Oprah's Internet series, aired live in 2008. I discovered significant insights that helped me gain a broader perspective about ego and its influential power if undetected or unchecked. This series also reinforced my belief that Oneness exists in all energy forms.

In earlier years, I tried to practice the Oneness philosophy, even when I didn't completely feel it at the time. Intuitively, I knew that I was sensing something and wanted to continue this practice. It is important to stretch ourselves to increase any desired effect, and not get discouraged by setbacks. Whenever I practiced Oneness, my energy aligned with the Bartholomew Effect, which I have experienced regularly. Often I have wondered if those of us on earth actually reach that place where we always feel Oneness with all life. I don't think so, yet that doesn't mean that we can't strive for it. The more that we focus on Oneness, the more it becomes our reality.

My hope is that we will embrace the "present moment" and "live in the now" as Tolle and other spiritual teachers have suggested. We can visualize a better world; commit to daily, quiet meditation or prayer times; and be active in our communities. Each of us is needed for this purpose right now. Let us join others who are already acting on this purpose and become Light Workers together.

The ultimate Truth of reality and spiritual awareness is convergence, not separation. Practicing nonjudgment is an important decision that leads to Oneness. We move forward when we respect and honor each individual's personal spiritual path.

We need to break through any boundaries that limit our thinking and perceptions. Deep in all of us is a universal consciousness. We would be wise to dedicate ourselves to attaining the highest awareness and potential for our soul's growth. Let us consider a shift in consciousness merely by staying open. Even though I am one seeker among many, it is my hope that some of the experiences and insights of my life's journey will increase readers' desire for awareness and exploration. It begins with trust.

Epilogue

Epilogue

Based on the research of Nita, who has a ministerial license with a master's degree in Comparative World Religions, I discovered that all religions seek a connection to a higher, divine source. I realized that each religion sees God uniquely and enters the journey with a different view of how to connect with God. Once I ventured beyond the dogma, rules, and tenets of various religions, I learned that there were more similarities among them than differences.

As people reach a certain level of awareness, I believe that most will desire to move beyond religion to a more inclusive spirituality or state of being. Recently I have moved to a new place of awareness. This pure unconditional love of the Christ Consciousness that I've encountered as Bartholomew is now a permanent resident in my heart and soul. This love is an all-accepting and an all-inclusive vibration of energy. It allows me to live in love and trust as I more fully realize that all is in divine order.

Now that you have witnessed the thoughts and experiences of my continuing spiritual journey, I bless you, my reader, with this same unconditional, all-accepting love of the heart. It is my hope that you will absorb more than the intellectual understanding of the words, that you will feel them in your heart. I imagine the vibration of unconditional love to permeate all levels of your being. I trust the awakening process will help you connect with the Divine, with the Christ Conscious energy, with each other, and with all of life. You will truly radiate Oneness.

Collection 1

Wisdom Questionnaire

Wisdom Questionnaire

Directions: Please answer the following questions.

1. Right now, if you were to leave your physical body through death, what is the most important wisdom you would share from your life experiences? (Please answer in *one or two sentences*.)

2. Specifically, how did you gain this wisdom? (Please answer in *one or two sentences*.)

For statistical purposes, please check the box or give a short answer that best describes you.

Age
☐ Under 20   ☐ 21-25   ☐ 26-30   ☐ 31-35
☐ 36-40   ☐ 41-45   ☐ 46-50   ☐ 51-55
☐ 56-60   ☐ 61-65   ☐ 66-70   ☐ 71-75
☐ 76-80   ☐ 81-85   ☐ 86-90   ☐ Over 90

Gender   ☐ M   ☐ F

Occupation

Other information/Spiritual affiliation

Collection 2

Meditations

Meditations

I wrote the following meditations in the early 1990's. The first meditation, "Wisdom from Within," is a culmination of the condensed wisdom of fifty people who completed my wisdom questionnaire. This is the same questionnaire that is located at the back of the book as Collection 1. You can also find the questionnaire on my web site, www.awakeningtooneness.com or contact Larry Vorwerk, P.O. Box 401, Northfield, MN 55057. Please submit your responses to the wisdom questionnaire before reading "Wisdom from Within" or other meditations that are located in Collection 2.

The other mediations were a result of my deep soul searching for meaning in life. I felt divinely inspired each time I wrote. It is best to find a relaxed, serene setting in which to read and contemplate the meaning of the meditations.

Meditation 1: Wisdom from Within*

Be at peace; don't take life too seriously; don't worry, roll with the punches. Maintain a sense of humor, for much joy in living is masked by worry. Try hard to enjoy your life because worry and stress are like rungs on a ladder: when you reach one rung, there is another one above it. Take stress situations in stride and learn from them to accomplish your next task. If your cross is too heavy, try lifting the one belonging to your neighbor. You won't want to trade.

Know and believe that all of the information you need to become who you are to become, is buried in the well of your own being. Take time to be still and to listen to your longings and your dreams. Allow them to speak to you and to create the life that you most desire. Trust yourself, and the indwelling Christ where all answers for you are personally available. Live your highest Truth and allow others to live theirs. Be open to what Love/God wishes to do through you.

Learn to know who you are. Believe in and be kind to yourself. Love yourself, and others will also love you. Be honest and sincere with yourself and others. Authentically express and live your beliefs and morals. Don't miss an opportunity to tell someone that you care.

So, walk softly through this world. From other species, learn the difference between needs and wants. Use your intellect as a gift, not a weapon. Try to help... try not to harm. Don't be convinced of, nor overburdened with your own importance. Learn to relax with nature, for nature in all its diversity and beauty is a great teacher and source of calm. God dwells within all forms of nature and within our hearts.

Don't be swayed by the pressures of others, rather allow your life to be determined by what lies within your heart. Be real. Be yourself. Don't try to be something or someone you're not. You are a child of God and are loved more than you can imagine. Give your heart to God, keeping alive and strong your faith and trust in Him. This day, celebrate your life and all of God's creation...for you are loveable, loved, and loving.

*Wisdom compiled from the 'Christ Within' fifty loving people, whose lifetimes tallied over 2,000 years of life experiences.

1991

Meditation 2: The Look of Love

How do you describe a power greater than any other power? It is the power of the look of love. This power is totally inclusive, encompassing all. It is a power even greater than the gravitational pull of a black hole. Within a black hole, that power is so strong that even light cannot escape from its force. However, the Look of Love is so strong that it reaches the distance of the farthest star in the most distant universe. Yet, it is closer than the distance between two atoms.

How powerful is the look of love? Look...really look lovingly...into the eyes of another person, and you will transcend all sense of space and time. The look of love encompasses all dimensions of space and time. The look of love, when two people's eyes meet, is an eternal experience, one in which love is seen in the mind's eye, as well. Although love transcends the five senses and is felt in the heart, the beauty of the physical senses can also add to the experience. Look lovingly into another's eyes, and when tears of love well up into those eyes, the tears add feelings to the experience of love, a movement of creation.

You ask, "Where is God?" Just look lovingly into the eyes of another person and you will be looking into the eyes of God, the eyes of Love. There is no quicker or more definite way to find God than to look with love into the eyes of another. When two people lovingly gaze into each other's eyes, they will see their way back Home to the Godhead, the source of our being. As God's love is reflected, they will see and experience the love of God within themselves.

We are all love, and the look of love says it all.

Action: Really look into the eyes of your loved one.

1993

Meditation 3: A Rare and Precious Gem in the "Sea of Humanity"

There once was a lad who was always searching...for what, he did not know. One day while walking along the shores of the "Sea of Humanity," he spotted a rare and precious gem in the rough, laying at the edge of the sea. Unlike all of the locals who visited the sea, he saw the true beauty which hid within the rough exterior of this rare and precious stone.

One of the most prized, valuable, and rare gems in the universe, this stone was a green diamond. The lad knew that green was the symbol of life and growth. How he wanted to pick up this diamond and take it home with him. He knew, though, that until the stone became polished, it would not truly shine forth all of its beauty and brilliance. Leaving it by the seashore, he knew the waves of life would slowly hone its rough edges.

The lad waited patiently day and night, year after year for the waves of life to carefully reveal the true beauty that was within the rare, precious stone. As more and more of the locals were illuminated by the light which radiated from the gem, the lad came to realize that he could never claim the gem for himself.

The gem was there for the benefit of all. He benefited from the light which radiated from this gem, and would take many trips to the Sea of Humanity to absorb the beauty of the gem. Over time, he realized that its beauty was actually his reflection and he had found what he was searching for: himself.

We are each a rare and precious gem in the Sea of Humanity. We have different facets, but when polished by the waves of life, we sparkle with the brilliance of a million stars, illuminating the world and all those around us. Acknowledge this precious gem that you are; be thankful for the waves of life, and shine forth this precious gift that you are—a light of love and beauty that only God could have created.

Action: You are a light in the world—shine forth—now and throughout eternity.

1994

Meditation 4: A Rare and Precious Gem in the "Sea of Humanity"—the Sequel

The lad took a quantum leap when he came to realize that he was also a green diamond, a rare and precious gem. The God/Love Light dwells within all gems. It is released as incoherent light, light that travels in different directions with various frequencies when we believe we are separated from each other.

When we practice Oneness, the God/Love Light is coherent light, light traveling in the same direction that combines with and amplifies the triggering light. The lad saw his reflection in another diamond, observing it to be similar to a laser. As the God/Love Light within the green diamond reflected back and forth, the light intensified and pierced the darkness where it had never reached before. Other gems caught the triggering light and joined the God/Love Light amplification. This chain reaction continued, until it spread throughout the entire Sea of Humanity.

A new dawn is rising in the Sea of Humanity as each critical gem takes a quantum leap, causing the phase transition on earth. All gems will experience the God/Love Light at a level of amplification never before felt on this planet. We will begin to realize that we are all rare and precious gems, reflecting the same God/Love Light. "Whatever we do unto others, we do unto ourselves." As such, earth will experience the love of God as it

was meant to be. We will live in an all-inclusive state of love.
Action: Take a quantum leap. Become a laser and live
in the unity and Oneness of God, now and throughout
eternity—as pure love—for that is what you truly are.

1994

Collection 3

I am Poems

I Am Poems

In the mid 1990's I went through a half-year period of writing my *I Am Poems*. These poems were created as I visualized life from the perspective of my high self. It was another way for me to expand my thinking of what life might look like from another state of consciousness. Most of these poems evolved from using the viewpoint of other life forms. I speculate on the probability that inanimate forms may have a sense of consciousness. May these poems help you see life and consciousness with new awareness.

An Alpine Spruce Needle Am I

An Alpine Spruce needle am I.
High above the valley floor sit I, precariously clinging to
    the rocky slopes of a barren wind-swept ridge.
I struggle so hard to stay attached to a twig, my support
    and lifeline.
In return, I convert the energy from the sun above to fuel
    my anchor, my life and my love.
How we work together day and night to beat the
    elements of wind, cold, and ice.
And yet someday, I must let go and surrender to the
    world below.
But until that day comes, I'll fight to stay as one.
An Alpine Spruce needle am I.

November 10, 1995

A Maple Leaf Am I

A Maple leaf am I.
A consciousness I have in me.
My purpose is to bring beauty to the world.
I grow in strength throughout the summer, so when the
    time is right, I may use my creative powers to display
    wondrous beauty.
As the air chills at summer's end, I send sugar down my
    veins.
The timing and proportions must be just right to create
    the colors and designs of heavenly delight.
Even though my sisters have colors of gold, red, yellow,
    orange and green, no two of us are quite the same.
To bring a smile of love and glee to a child of thee is the
    greatest purpose for me.
A Maple leaf am I.

November 10, 1995

The Frost Am I

The frost am I.
During a cold, calm, dark night, I appear.
I form a feathery, crystalline structure.
My brothers and I line up on every available space, on
    every twig of a great dormant pine.
We then wait for our moment of glory.

As morning breaks, the sun appears above the horizon.
We transmute our brother, the tree, into a radiant being.
The transformed pine dances with a rainbow of lights, as
    it sways gently in the morning breeze.

A human appears on the scene to gaze upon this radiant
    being.
The love and beauty of God is mirrored to the mind of
    this divine being, as he takes in the beauty of the radi-
    ant lights of the transformed pine.
His love and warmth changes my crystalline structure.
I let go of my clingy perch and gently float toward the
    ground.
The love and warmth I feel excite me, and I evaporate
    into the surrounding air.

I now become one with the surrounding air, the world
    around me, the human, and my God.
I have delivered the message I was created for.
We are all One.
I am pleased. My God is pleased.
For I am. We are.
The frost am I.

February 9, 1996

A Slug Am I

A slug am I.
A simple consciousness have I.
My life is simple without clutter.
I go about my daily life, all movements purposeful and deliberate.
I feel secure and at peace, for I know that I am loved and cared for by my Creator.
To rush about would be a denial of that awareness.
As such, I have all the time in the world to be what I am.
I live in the eternal now, for time is almost meaningless for me.
To live this way is to honor my God.
You may think that I am but a mindless, simple creature, but am I?
A slug am I.

March 29, 1996

The Fog Am I

The fog am I.
My consciousness is one of envelopment.
On calm, humid nights, I descend on valleys below.
I bring all of life unto myself as I embrace it into my
form.
My moist kiss caresses the cheeks of a jogger, the petal of
a flower, the bud of a tree, the wings of a butterfly, and
the rough outcropping of a stony crevice.
I do not place judgment on any of these life forms, for I
take them all unto myself as One.
All of their thoughts and feelings become One with mine,
as we become connected through all that I am.
Oh, how blessed I am to be able to feel this Oneness with
all that I envelop.
It is truly a gift of my Creator to be so loved.
Feel the love and Oneness that we all are.
The fog am I.

March 29, 1996

A Fragrance Am I

A fragrance am I.
I am that which simulates your senses.
My power is great.
I cause you to recall the illusions of your past, the dreams
    of your future, and the bliss of the moment.

I enhance your life.
With me, you may truly celebrate the divine being that
    you are.
Recall my fragrance. It is of the autumn leaves, moist
    with dew in the depth of a deciduous forest;
That of the essence of a lover, caressed in your arms as
    you join in Oneness in thought and in body;
That of a scented rose, the most aromatic of flowers,
    which helps you transcend this world as you sense
    the presence of Mother Mary, the mother of Jesus.

Know that I have been given as a gift to you.
For with me, you truly can experience the wonders of this
    world.
This world is your playground.
A world of your creation.
A world of beauty and awe.
Rejoice in me.
For I am the essence of the heavenly realm.
The bliss of your creativity.
The power of your mind.
A fragrance am I.

April 7, 1996

A Musical Note Am I

A musical note am I.
I am the vibration within the silence.
Without the silence, I would be nothing more than a
    vibration of noise.
With the silence, I am of the highest vibration known to man.
The silence and I are One, for we are in harmony with
    each other.

I fill your world with beauty and love.
To know me, is to long for me, to love me.
Love and I are interchangeable.

I am the manifestation of your most loving thoughts and
    desires.
I am the chorus of frogs, the chatter of migrating grack-
les, the roar of the sea, the howl of the wind, the melody
    of the harp, and the laughter of a child.
Of these, the highest musical note of all is laughter.
Laughter is the vibration of joy, of love, of Oneness.
A truly divine musical note.

It is I who unites your lower self with your God self.
Call on me, and know that you are in the presence of
    your God, for we are united in the great I AM.
A musical note am I.

April 7, 1996

A Gnat Am I

A gnat am I.
An Attention-getter am I.
My small size shouldn't fool you.
The power I have over you will amaze you.

You may wonder why I even exist.
If you knew, it may remake your entire world anew.
Swarms of us may annoy you, but not in such a way as
    when one of us makes a supreme sacrifice, and finds a
    way into your eye.

Think of the control of your concentration that is on me
    when I am in your eye.
A little gnat that I am has your full attention.
To think that a divine being, a God like you, would focus
    all of your attention on me, a little gnat.
How important that makes me feel, especially when there
    are so many other things on which you could focus
    your attention and spend your time.

You, being a co-creator with God, have the power to
    direct your intentions on anything you so choose.
You can create laughter, joy, and happiness in all those
    around you just by the focus of your smile or a kind
    word.
You can create amazing things by centering your mind on
    your body as you create beautiful music or great works of art.
Most of all, you can create love, with the concentration of
    your intentions, emulating from your heart.

This love that you create can be shared with whomever
   or whatever you so desire.
So, remove me with love the next time I land in your eye.

Then direct your next intentions in loving, creative ways.
Oh, I'm so happy I caught your attention.
Now you know why I exist.
A gnat am I.

April 30, 1996

Collection 4

As an Eagle Soars

As the Eagle Soars

As the Eagle Soars entitles that part of my spiritual journal written from the mid-1990s to 2000. Mostly, these are additional personal reflections and insights that contributed to my spiritual development. I included particular entries where the themes were universal.

Agape Love

I would like to share some examples that illustrate my understanding of how to experience heaven/love/the Christ Consciousness on earth.

Dave, a mutual friend of ours, visited us just before Christmas. At the end of our evening of enjoyable conversation, we went outside and began talking again. Nita must have come outside at one point and, seeing how much Dave and I were taking pleasure in the conversation, said from her heart, "I love you both."

At that moment, I felt total bliss because I was emotionally connected to both of them. Dave and I were at a place of harmony in our discussion. Soon I picked up the following feelings from Nita, "I deeply care for each of you, and it brings me great joy to see you two enjoying each other's company." I was delighted to see Nita's visible joy in observing the agreeable conversation between Dave and me.

The three of us were as One. There was no separation of feelings among us. I saw and felt only the God self of love in each of us. That state of bliss lasted but a few moments, yet can be recaptured whenever I so choose.

Think of the level of love/agape love that can be experienced when we share that Oneness of love with our family members, community, country and world. All of us would be vibrating at the same level.

Sadly, society tells us that not everyone can be loved equally. An example is how society views relationships involving gay, lesbian, or bisexual individuals. Also consider polygamous relationships and other relationships besides the acceptable traditional monogamous relationships. Love and its vibration is not dependant on sexuality. Love is the same regardless of who receives it or how it is expressed. The beauty of group love is that the experience of agape love increases exponentially as the number of individuals increases. I continue to focus on a more inclusive experience of love with all people and life forms I encounter.

The experience of love comes from within, for that

is where God resides. The level of love we want to experience comes from within. It is our choice. Throughout this Christmas season, I share and radiate all of the love that I am to each of you who means so much to me. Experience the same love that brings greater understanding.

December 30, 1995

As the Eagle Soars

Creation of Reality

As in all of my spiritual writings of *As the Eagle Soars*, I try to take others further into my experiences and understanding of reality. A powerful experience occurred yesterday, and I feel that I should pass it on.

Nita and I attended the final session of the Eleventh Annual Symposium of the International Institute of Integral Human Sciences, held in River Falls, Wisconsin. Using the theme *Creating Community—Our Journey Home*, this six-day symposium/retreat focused on global, personal and spiritual development. We attended lectures, workshops, and informal discussions while experiencing cultural diversity and participating in events designed to assist our personal journeys of self-discovery.

The day began with a keynote lecture combined with special musical selections. After that, we chose to attend different morning workshops. I attended Steven McFadden's workshop entitled, "Pilgrims on a Path of Fire:

Healing Ourselves and the Earth." Steven stated, "In ancient times, people often set out on a pilgrimage for penance, as well as to gain the blessings of holy places. Today, the pilgrimage was taking on a different character. Pilgrims often journeyed into nature, as well as to the great sacred sites of the earth, not specifically for themselves, but to direct their prayers and intentions in support of a gravely-ill Earth Mother."

Such pilgrimages often sparked dramatic advances in personal growth and development. With breath, sound, story, discussion, walking meditations and a mystery journey, we explored and mastered a range of critical teachings on pilgrimage and soul growth. We learned a variety of techniques for engaging sacred sites and also explored the life journeys of several pilgrims. As a group, we hoped to orient our steps rightly to the present and the future.

Steven took fourteen of us around the college campus for a guided walking meditation and mystery journey of a classic seven-circuit labyrinth. We explored the use of this powerful tool for prayer, personal balance and spiritual insight.

In preparation for this meditation, we were first smudged with sage and told about how things of nature, such as feathers, were messengers. Common to many Native American traditions, the four directions were used in this meditation. As we became part of the meditation, we first lay in the north direction and were guided to ask: Spirit, who am I? The answer I received: I am like a synapse. We are a world and even a universe within, and we're ourselves. We are also just like a synapse, within a larger body, Mother Earth, which is part of a larger universe. The key to being a synapse is that we always have free will to create new pathways for the Love energy (God/Source) that pass through us by focusing on that Love energy.

Next, we lay facing east and were guided to ask: Spirit, why am I here? The answer I received: You are here to experience and help others to experience the Christ Consciousness on earth, as it is in the spiritual world. Little did I know that I would witness an amazing event within a few, short minutes.

Then we lay facing south and were guided to ask: Spirit, what is my next step? The answer I received was both profound and simple: Take a step forward.

Finally we lay facing west. We were told to lie in silence and wait to learn of the Great Mystery. This I interpreted as waiting to receive the grand meanings of life. As we felt moved, we were to get up and walk through the labyrinth while in meditation for the Great Mystery.

As I got up and began to walk through the labyrinth, I was suddenly encouraged to pick up a small pinecone from the ground. The voice of Spirit Within told me that this pinecone was a gift to me from the pine tree. At first

I thought I would keep this pinecone, along with other special nature gifts.

I was told that I was to pass on the pinecone. I was told that we experience the Christ Consciousness when we are of service to others. "For it is in giving that we receive," as the Bible states. It is when we demonstrate selfless giving that we experience Love/Oneness or the Christ Consciousness which is all inclusive and multidimensional.

I was then told to give my pinecone as a gift to the woman who was walking behind me on the labyrinth. I had not seen her nor did I know her, so I slowed my steps until she caught up to me. Placing one hand on the tree, the source of the pinecone, I offered the woman the pinecone.

The woman also placed one of her hands on the same pine tree while accepting my gift of a pinecone. I then felt called to hug her in recognition that we are all One. I was truly at One with the woman, the pine tree and the world around me. I now knew the Great Mystery.

After completing the meditation, I approached the woman to share with her the full story of my experience. It was then that I learned she was the editor of the *Turtle River Press*—a publication of creative energy. Another example of serendipity: a poem from my *I Am Collection* had been published in a recent edition of her publication.

Are these instances just coincidental? I don't think

so. Each person will need to decide. The labyrinth experiences of each participant were different, resulting in real and meaningful events. We do create our own reality. It is my desire to help create a world of Love and Oneness on this earth. This directive is becoming my reality. What reality do you want to create?

August 10, 1997

As the Eagle Soars

Intense Gratitude and Love

Recently I was fortunate to experience a profoundly deep and intense feeling of gratitude at a level that I had never known. This experience has given me meaningful insights. I desire now to also share my feelings of gratitude and love for all the people and gifts that have come into my life.

I sensed this deep feeling of gratitude during a transmission meditation that occurred at the end of the meeting of our Spiritual Transformation Group. Nita conducted the transmission meditation which focused on healing the earth through spiritual beings. By concentrating on our highest intent, we acted as conduits for the spiritual realms to send their loving, healing energies to connect with Mother Earth. Generally, the transmission meditation occurred during a thirty-minute, silent meditative state set to soft, background music.

On this particular evening, the meditation started like most others. After a short while, I began to feel intense energy coursing through my body. Higher spiritual beings radiated an abundance of unconditional love to Mother Earth. I shed uncontrollable tears that patterned themselves after a river running down a mountainside, cleansing the earth as they flowed.

In response, I was able to feel Mother Earth sending out waves upon waves of gratitude and love. This unconditional exchange with the higher spiritual beings was nothing less than pure ecstasy!

The experience seemed to combine the gratitude of all sentient beings on planet earth. Everything and everyone experienced love at a higher level. Earth energies and spiritual beings evolved through the wholeness of pure, unconditional love. Yes, I was only an observer in all of this, yet because I was a conduit, I experienced all that took place.

I came away from this experience with a feeling that on a higher level all is well with our Mother. We can each do our part to help Mother Earth on a physical level. To Mother Earth, or the Gaia energy, we are like cells in her body.

I appreciate my connection with Spirit, earth and all of humanity. I feel grateful for having you in my life. May we continue to share our spiritual awareness and gratitude for life in its multitude of forms.

May 1, 2000

As the Eagle Soars

Heightened Communication and Harmony with Nature in the New Millennium

Recently Nita and I attended a Lammas-Tide Wedding of my friend, Tom and his new wife, Alison. Set in a beautiful Wisconsin valley with rolling, forested hills, the ceremony took place next to a pond. A mighty oak tree spread its canopy of draping foliage over the wedding party and guests, providing a graceful tent. Just before the ceremony began, a storm passed through the area. All were concerned that the service would be rained out. Nature knew better. She was just heralding the celebration.

The rain stopped—perfectly-timed by nature—and we witnessed the opening of the ceremony. Soon the sun started to peak ever so slightly through the clouds. There was a freshness to the land—a feeling of new beginnings and hope for brighter times. Tom and Alison chose readings and songs that honored their love and connection with nature. During the many years that I've known Tom, he has always loved trees.

This day the giant oak didn't forget him. As we sat in chairs under its abundant branches and leaves, I became emotionally overwhelmed. The tree communicated to me how proud it felt to play such a great role in the wedding.

As it shook rain drops to the guests below, the droplets of water transformed into droplets of love. The loving presence of the tree raised the vibration of the surrounding area. The loving feelings of the wedding party also contributed to this heightened vibration.

Not to be left out, the rest of nature came to gift its presence to the occasion. Distant songbirds sang lovely melodies throughout the ceremony while fish jumped to indicate their presence. As Alison read her poem of love for Tom, "If I Called You River," the pond became quiet. While Tom read his poem of love for Alison, "Earth Song," the sun fully displayed its radiance. When it was time to repeat their vows and exchange rings, gentle breezes carried their words across the valley and to the far reaches of the universe.

As guests felt Tom and Alison's deep love for each other, Nature also expressed its deep love for each of us. We were in harmony and felt the love and higher vibration of a world in a new millennium. We are able to create this world of love, harmony and higher communication with nature. I am beginning to understand how it will become more and more common to experience this level of awakening as we move further into the millennium.

By adding your creative love to this beautiful earth, indeed, we will be able to call it heaven on earth.

August 8, 2000

Collection 5
Internal Messages of Wisdom

Internal Messages of Wisdom

I wrote numerous Internal Messages of Wisdom over a two-year period. Shortly after my sessions of past life recall as Bartholomew, I received internal messages from Jesus. Other beings also wanted to share insights with me. Since I had included information from the Wisdom Questionnaires, I thought it would give readers a more comprehensive view if additional wisdom from the great teachers of the Other Side was also included.

Insights came through to me from many teachers on the other side of the veil. These messages were more complete and multidimensional than I personally could have written. I hope this wisdom from a multidimensional realm will provide greater clarity.

Christmas Message

Dear Son,

We are in the Christmas season, a time that was always blessed to me. We see it somewhat differently here on this side of the veil. It is a time to reflect on our own Christ Consciousness—a time to see where we reflect our own God empowerment. We now know that we are so much more than we were led to believe while in human form.

The key is to become aware of your Christ Consciousness while in human form. There is so much more you can accomplish with this awareness when in human form. How you accomplish this on earth has far-reaching effects, and can influence even those aspects of yourself that are not in human form or are of other worlds.

This is why there is so much interest in humanity at this juncture of time. The knowingness that you take on is what is important. This knowingness comes mainly from intent. You don't even have to be exposed to the knowledge directly. It is through intent that you draw knowledge to you. Knowledge is nothing more than awareness, for all knowledge is available to you.

The greatest knowledge, though, is pure love. This is the love that resides in your heart. It is through the intent of pure love that all things are possible. It is important to realize that pure love is unconditional love. That means that your intent is all-inclusive. As such, you are drawn outside of yourself to see the good of the whole.

As you reach out to others, you are reaching out to yourself. For it is in giving that we receive. So this Christmas season, find the Christ within and give to others so that in return, you might receive. It is a season of giving. The greatest gift you can give is your Christ Consciousness. For only then can you truly give to the world what the world needs most, the peace and love of self-realization. We are each God, experiencing the love of self when we become self-actualized as the love of the One. Love and peace, son, is my gift to you this Christmas season.

Dad

December 5, 2004

Expressive Consciousness

Yes, I do have something to say. I am Tom, a soul who had been on your earth in the last century. You are so restrictive in expressing yourselves while in human form. Know that you are all truly much more expressive when not in the cloaking of human flesh. It is so nice to be in any location, unconfined to a body while expressing myself in all ways. Soon you will have this opportunity to become more expressive as you ascend and raise your vibration.

More senses will be available to you, senses that have been dormant for so long. Senses come in many forms. When you are made aware of them, you can activate them. This includes the ability to alter your consciousness, enabling multidimensional travel. In fact, that is how you can hear me now.

This ability will enrich your lives. It is through multidimensional travel that you will bring Home to earth. Meditation is one form of changing consciousness, but there are easier and quicker ways available. This is made possible because your vibration and the earth's vibration have increased. The key is to become quiet and use focus and intent as you go within.

All worlds exist within you. The outer world isn't anything more than the projection of your inner world. People are a universe within themselves. Knowing that all worlds really exist within you makes it possible to change consciousness. When your intent is to go within someone else's consciousness, you have no control there. But when you focus within yourself, then all the power and control is with and within you. It is when two or more people go within themselves and join in consciousness that demonstrates Jesus' statement, 'When two or more of you join in my name, there am I.' When you feel love and go within, that is when and how you connect in love with others.

All worlds exist within. As the saying goes 'Like attracts like.' With this awareness, you can step outside of time and connect instantly with any souls you want. If the focus and intent of their vibration is similar to yours, you will be in instant communication. It is with this awareness that telepathy will become a common form of communication in the years ahead. Practicing telepathy will be similar to fine-tuning a radio station, locating your frequency of choice. Everyone's thoughts are flowing through the airwaves. Now you will know how to tune into each other's frequency to hear and communicate your thoughts.

Many souls on this side of the veil are more than willing to share knowledge of how to use other senses in telepathy. They are just as eager to interact with you on a conscious level as you are with them. This will happen in time. I appreciate the opportunity to come through to you now. I've been waiting in line a long time. In the future, there will be many souls available to you. Right now there are many more on my side of the veil who want to connect with souls in human form than there are human souls willing to connect. Blessings to you and for the work you are about to do.

Tom

December 20, 2004

The Language of Love

Love is what I want to speak of today. Do you feel my love? That is the language you will speak in the new world. It is truly a language all of its own. Love does not need to be spoken, for it permeates all of life. Love can be felt in the heart chakra. When souls raise their vibrations to a higher level, they can start to speak the language of love. Since love permeates everything, it is all-inclusive of words and feelings.

Love combines the meaning of words and feelings together. This is why it is a more accurate language than the spoken word. Those who speak from the heart with pure intention are constantly communicating with others, regardless if they are conscious of the communication. The language of love is a harmonious energy vibration. Love is the language of interconnection at the deepest level because love carries the highest vibration.

When a message is received in love, it is one's soul seeing itself in another soul. If you could see all of your communication exchanges with others as self-expressed love, you would see the world differently. You would see the interconnection of all life. When that realization occurs, an amazing thing happens. There is instant communication between all parts of the whole of life. Once that happens, verbal communication may no longer be needed because the vibration of love is nonverbal. Even though the message received may not speak directly of love, the carrier of the message is love. Love carries the highest vibration.

Earth is ascending now. We are aware of any vibration of love more easily. You will see love expressed more and more as your earth ascends. As time goes on, it will become easier for you to express love. When earth and its inhabitants reach a certain level of vibration, amazing things will happen. Energy will be expressed through a creative mode, instead of through a survival mode. Currently, your earth is expressing itself mainly in survival mode. You can choose another path. Pure love is the highest form of creative, divine expression.

'You are the one you have been waiting for.' You don't need to save yourself from anything except the illusions you have created. I know you've heard of this in some form or another, yet maybe not in this same vibration. The way words are grouped together activates a different vibration. May this message bring a little different view of what love truly is and what it can do.

I have had many lifetimes on your earth, yet I see myself as each of you. To say that I am *this person* or *that person* is too limiting. I am much more, just as you are. We are all expressions of LOVE. (Note: This felt like a male energy.)

A Nameless Being

January 3, 2005

Mother Earth

Peace. Be still. Hear your breath. The rhythm is the same as the earth. You are One, you and the earth. You and humanity are entering a time when you will know that awareness. It is a time when humanity will treat the earth as itself. Even though each soul has its own identity, it is also part of Mother Earth. You live and breathe as One. For, in your greater reality, you are One. Just as a blood cell within your body has its own life, it is also an intricate part of your body and your life. As you ascend, you will become more aware of your greater self. Just as you become aware that you are a part of Mother Earth, your individual cells will become aware of their connections to you.

This is why you can talk to your cells and expect a change in your physical body. Your cells' best interests align with what is in your best interest regarding your health and well-being. More information and knowledge will be given to you in the future about working directly with your own bodies. There will be additional direct communication between your cells and your greater self—the personality and soul.

As humanity experiences that interconnection between all things, humanity will start to interact with all of life as an intricate part of itself. When this happens, all of life will change dramatically. At that time you will see yourselves as the center of the universe again—which you are. The difference is now you will see the whole universe as part of you. Previously, you viewed the rest of the universe as being outside of you. As such, it was you against the universe. Now it will be the entire universe working together for the good of the whole, in which your physical body and soul are intricate parts of the universe. You will never truly feel alone again, for how could you?

You are fully connected and supported by all of life. Life could be described as God. For life and God are One—just as you are One with and in God. With this awareness will come the conscious effort to work with and support all of life, a natural and effortless outcome. The result will be a life of harmony and cooperation between kingdoms. All kingdoms on your earth are like organs in the body. They are distinct entities, yet are important and must work together for the greater good of the whole. The difference now will be the greater awareness of how intricately intertwined we are with all of life. Knowledge and awareness is the key ingredient here. That knowledge and awareness only comes in the form of a higher vibration. For the higher the vibration, the greater and more expansive is the knowledge and awareness. They go hand in hand. You will come to know what ascension is really all about. It is truly the experience and awareness of the Oneness of all life, which is love.

I am the consciousness of Mother Earth.

January 9, 2005

Color

Color.....Blue.....Your earth is a blue planet. Humanity will start to pay more attention to color as a vibration. As vibrations rise, you will be aware of more meaning in the colors you see and experience. Since everything is energy, which gives off a certain vibration, all things produce a color. Color comes in more expressions of vibrations than you can imagine. In fact, there are more colors and shades than there are words in your English language.

When you look at something, pay more attention to its color. Color gives added meaning to everything. Spiritual beings in your presence send out a radiant hue of colors to make their presence known. As you move into the new earth reality, you will start to see the shadow-like colors of these beings. The vibration of colors they release will change according to their thoughts, feelings and expressions. This is why higher-evolved spiritual beings have such radiant auras. This is an expression of who and what they are.

Their radiant expressions of color send an internal message. This is another way to communicate telepathically with others. Receive their colors and express your own colors by intentional vibration. These colors I speak of are seen internally, so it makes no difference if you are physically blind or not. This is one of the many other senses that humanity is noticing and starting to develop.

Color has a language all of its own. Color can be used to heal, communicate, express, and even to merge with others. When you vibrate at the same color frequency as another, then you merge. All that you are and all that another is joins as One. This is what happened to you, Larry, as you encountered the group-mind experience years ago. In order for that to happen, fear could not be part of your vibrations at that moment. It is love that brings individual colors together in unison and harmony.

Love is an ever-changing, expressive color, with unlimited hues. Its radiance is noticeably different from colors that are lacking a vibration of love. This is another way you can sense a person's intent. At any given moment, a person's aura will express in color the true intention or state of expression of that individual. Colors do not lie. They are as unique as a person's fingerprints.

You are eternally known for your colors. As you grow and change, your colors will change. More accurately, colors are added to you as you become more radiant in your light and expression. You are all light beings, radiating your own unique colors throughout the universe. Be the radiant light being that you are. You are loved for your colors.

Zackryon, a Being of Color

January 23, 2005

Living in a Changed World

I am Earl. I have wanted to come to you for a long time. I am here to say that you have arrived. You are living the ascended life on the new earth. It will take some time for humanity to fully realize this. It will come in slow, yet sudden realizations, as you see your world change from the inside out.

First, you will notice the changes within yourselves. You will know that your world isn't the world you were born into. There will be a sense of magnetism between your inner and outer worlds. By this I mean you will see how your thoughts and actions intersect, or are a part of, others' thoughts and actions. You will begin to lose that sense of separation between your actions and others' actions. It will happen in such a way that you may not even perceive the change. This is good because it will be a gradual, natural process.

As more and more of humanity start to live this reality, your outer world will have to change. It already has. If you were to look at issues of how people separate themselves from each other compared to how they are inclusive, you will see that people are more inclusive than not. You might believe otherwise only because of what is shown in your media systems. By-and-large, what people view are those concepts from the old energy system that currently control your media. They are continuing to make a last ditch effort to perpetuate the notion of separation through your programs and advertisements. This is soon to change. In fact it is changing now.

You will soon see a major change in the format of newscasts and message delivery. As this happens, people will wake up and realize that they have been duped. Once the media (and I speak about all forms of the media that reach large audiences) change their focus to one of support, encouragement, connectedness, progress, and enhancement of humanity and life, people will realize their true nature. That true nature is one of connectedness, unity, love base, and support of the greater good of the whole.

As humanity awakens, more knowledge and wisdom will readily be available for the enhancement of your newly evolving world. The focus of your resources, including your financial resources, will shift. More and more resources will be used to further the uplifting of humanity. This is especially true in your third world countries. These resources will heal your environment, with new knowledge and understanding of methods and devices to heal your earth.

Support will come from the most unlikely places and sources. Think outside of the box now. Your world is a lot larger than you had believed in the past. As the earth and your vibrations continue to rise, more and more life will appear in your physical reality. There will be a grand reunion of your brothers and sisters. You are truly living a broader reality now. Wake up and realize it. Rejoice in what you have accomplished and celebrate in the grandness of life.

This is Earl, formerly Earl of Lexingburg

January 30, 2005

We Are Each a Part of the Whole

I am Brandy, a light being, who comes to you this day. We are all loved for who we are. To love our Truth, to be the essence of who we are, is our greatest mission. For each soul is unique and important. Each soul holds all of life together. No one soul is more important than another. Each soul has the same power in the greater reality of life and can exist in many realities, or universes, at the same time.

What you do in this world at this time has far-reaching effects throughout creation. It is a time in human evolution that is critical for the direction of your universe. If all of humanity were aware of this, how different your world would be. To be that which you truly are is your journey. It is an awareness that is finally starting to take hold in human consciousness.

The power of Source is within each soul. It always has been this way and always will be. The power of your mind is a great and powerful thing. All of the powers of creation are within each and every one of you. Each thought creates another universe, or potential universe of existence. You are beings that create universes within universes. Life exists in all directions.

Your awareness of this universe is only one island in this sea of reality you call life. Regardless of how small, it still interacts with all of the greater expansions of life.

With this awareness, comes the realization of the value and impact of your thoughts, words, and actions on all life forms. You are a key player. You are the alpha and the omega. And yet, so is every other soul. This is the Oneness of all of life.

There are many ways to explain unity and interconnection. The key is not how you explain it, but how you know it. To know Oneness at your core, that you are one with all of life, you acknowledge Oneness in all of your thoughts, words, and actions.

When you live in the harmony of Oneness, you are living a life of love, joy, fulfillment, and peace. The time of the illusion of separation is leaving your global consciousness. A new world is being born. This is a new world of greater understanding of the greater reality. This new understanding will create the wondrous world that will rise above the horizon of your awareness. You are birthing this new world. Be proud and own the God/Goddess within you that is capable of such a wondrous creation. Live in the unity of Oneness that is love. This is my wisdom I share with you today.

I am Brandy. I am you.

February 6, 2005

Love on Valentine's Day

Love—this is a day of love. Love has many expressions and outlets. It is truly what makes the world turn. Earth was created as an expression of love. This may not be what you believe you see in the world today, but that belief is an illusion. If your world were not mainly an expression of love, it could not exist. If you truly want to live in a world of love, then expect it in your life and focus on it in everything you see and do.

Planet earth is a world of love. If you aren't experiencing it as such, then it is only because you choose not to see it. You will experience only what you expect to see. You are the creator of your reality. Each individual has a personal reality. Many see world expressions of fear (wars, anger, mistrust, isolation, despair, rejection, hatred). But if the truth be known, there are far more expressions of love in your world than you might realize.

Take a moment to think about what love might look like. It is love expressed as a thought. That thought is as real as an action of love. Thoughts are energy. Your earth is nothing less than an expressive thought of energy, and that thought is one of creative love. You increase the vibration of earth with each loving thought you express, with each loving action you engage in, and with each loving feeling that passes through your body.

The earth and all of its inhabitants will rise through the fourth dimension and into the fifth dimension because there are more loving vibrations on your earth. This change occurs only when love is the predominate vibration.

The energy of love is increasing. You can continue this process by focusing on love vibrations than on those of fear. The statement, 'fear feeds upon fear' is true; however, 'love also feeds upon love.' On this Valentine's Day, as on every day, feed love with more love. A world of love and peace will become your ever-expanding reality. This is truly a lovely planet.

More forms of life exist on your earth than you can imagine. All of these forms are expressing love in ways that they understand. Are you awake enough to see all of these expressions of love? Have hope and joy, for that time is soon approaching. As all life forms increase their vibrations, love will be easier to witness. All life has a God-given right to exist and express that love that they are. Honor that right.

Honor your Mother Earth, the womb of your birth and the nurturer of your heart. Remember, we are all One. The sooner we realize it, the sooner we will each experience the fulfillment of all life, fully expressing the love of the Creator. When all of creation is respected and honored, love will be fully expressed. That expression will happen sooner or later. Why not sooner? Live your life in love and harmony, and life will give you love and harmony.

I am Lilly, a being of love from your inner world of nature. I speak for the elementals on your planet.

February 14, 2005

Brothers in the Fifth Dimension

You are balls of pure light, pulsating at speeds of incredible brilliance as you radiate pure, divine love. Your true nature is this incredible state of being. All who look upon you are mesmerized by your wholeness. You reflect other souls in the day-to-day mirroring of life. Your lives are so much more than the human consciousness is capable of grasping.

Rejoice! Humanity is awakening to this greater reality of expanded awareness. Reality is the expansion of your dimensions of consciousness. A good way to look at this is to imagine humanity living in a two-dimensional world, a plane of length and width but no depth. Your world would seem very limited in this two-dimensional state. By comparison, moving to a fifth-dimensional world and looking back to a three-dimensional world would make you feel just as limited.

It takes time to adjust to a greater reality. When you move into the fifth dimension, part of your reality is to leave your consciousness of space and time. You are moving into no time, or all time that exists in the eternal now. In this state of consciousness, your reality is greatly expanded. You will be able to make marked progress in evolution. With experiences from all lifetimes available to your conscious mind, you will have a vast amount of information that you will easily process, resulting in better life decisions. Another aspect of this awareness will be your assessment of others' experiences, providing information to make the best decisions.

As you fully realize your fifth-dimensional status, you will know and experience connectedness with others. In this state, only love will exist in your consciousness. No fear will keep you separate. Without separation, you will not experience wars or other means of division as you live fully in the fifth dimension. You will truly understand the meaning of the phrase, 'There is only One of us on this planet.' It will be an incredible time of love and peace. There will be harmony among all parts of the whole of humanity.

As the one called Larry writes this, he is also experiencing the emotion of what he is writing. It is through the emotional experience that you come to understand the full meaning of the words expressed. I Come as a Brother, A Remembrance of Illusions* offers a greater understanding of the word brother. You are both brother and sister to another. This statement goes beyond humanity, and is true of all life. This experience is what humanity has to look forward to in the times ahead. Shed tears of joy, for you are all One.

This is Larry, Bartholomew, and Jesus the Christ, all as One in the brotherhood of humanity.

*Note: *I Come as a Brother, A Remembrance of Illusions* is a book about Bartholomew that was channeled and written by Mary-Margaret Moore.

February 28, 2005

Transformation

Transformation is what is happening on your planet at this time. It is the transformation of the whole. All parts of the whole are being transformed. The emergence of the butterfly is at hand. Just as it isn't possible for part of the butterfly to emerge while other parts stay as a caterpillar, so is it true with humanity. All of humanity who has chosen to ascend will do so. Those who have made the choice not to ascend will leave and go to other appropriate realms.

The time of waiting is over. The time of decision-making has ended. Those who have made the decision to ascend will know each other. Assistance in this process is overwhelmingly positive. The heavenly realms are at hand in this assistance. Once the emerging process starts (and it has), there is no stopping it. Do not doubt yourselves. You are ascending. If you are hearing or reading these words, you are among those ascending in this place and time.

Feel the vibration of the ascending process. The air is electrified. The actual process is rapid. Upon awakening to ascension, all can feel their connection to each other. You are no longer caterpillars that only can crawl on the ground. You are all butterflies that can fly wherever your hearts desire. Just as a school of fish moves in unison, so will the ascended souls move in unison as they create for the good of the whole.

Lives as butterflies are nothing like lives as caterpillars, and so it is with you. Dream big; dream in unison; dream for the good of the whole. You will create a dream world. You will create heaven on earth. This is your destiny. This is your God-given right. This is your true state of being, as co-creators with God.

Just as a butterfly doesn't think about what it has to do next to emerge from its chrysalis, so it is with you. Relax; let the process of ascension happen naturally. Don't force it. You will naturally draw to you the people and the situations you will need to ascend. See the beauty in the process. Enjoy the experience. Other realms of beings, light beings, will appear in your vision and in your reality.

No longer will you feel separate from all of life, for you are part of all of life. This is the great joy, the feeling of union. 'I know union' will be your motto. It will be your way of life. Union is reality. Separation is the illusion. You are leaving the world of illusion and ascending into a world of reality. Now go out and create a world of reality. You are all loved beyond comprehension. You are love eternal, with all of the love of the heavenly realms.

This is Archangel Gabriel.

March 3, 2005

An Open Heart

Love to humanity is the thought for today. I pour out my love to all as they journey in a time of change. Purity of heart is the cleansing that is taking place. Humanity's heart is being opened. This heart-felt world has not yet truly materialized on earth, until now. Many changes are taking place on earth.

Opening the heart is the greatest of these changes. It is with the heart opening that true love will be expressed. As the heart opens, love pours out. As love pours out, hearts become connected, and connected hearts function as one. The good of all is expressed as the function of a single heart of humanity. Humanity knows the necessity of air and water; it is what keeps you alive in your physical world.

In the new world that you create, love will be the enhanced element that will permeate your world. You will be living in a sea of love that will flow around and through you. It will be this sea of love that will raise your vibration. It will electrify the air you breathe and the water you drink.

An enhanced vision will be yours. Your world will sparkle and shine in ways never before seen on your earth. This vision will come from within the open heart of each and every person. For each open heart will see the glory of

God, of Source, beginning within and shining outward. All forms of energy in your newly-created world will reflect that glory.

That inner knowing of Source will be magnified. The needs of others will be known without speaking. An open heart will respond to that need. Humanity will respond to the needs of all in a loving way. As needs are met, humanity's focus will change to one of creation and joy. With enhanced connection to Source, greater forms of creation will be yours to be expressed.

You will live in the moment as you create in joy. Each moment in time will be a creative expression of Source. You will create your heaven on earth. With your heightened connection to Source, there will be no limit to your creations. The time is now, for now is the only time there ever has been. Open your heart to this awareness. The earth is your playground. Create in joy as the divine creation that you are.

This is from the Rose of Love,
Mother Mary

March 21, 2005

You Are the Creators of Your World

"Lost in space," meaning that you do not know where you are going, is a saying that is appropriate to many on earth. Even though your future is unknown, you have the capability to create it with your all-powerful thoughts.

The power of creation lies within. The Bible states, "As you think, so shall you become." Your world is a hologram of all your thoughts and your feelings. There is an inner world and an outer world. Your inner world is your personal thoughts and feelings. Your outer world is a collective group consciousness of thoughts and feelings. Without a collective consciousness that involves all of humanity, your outer world would cease to exist.

We feed into the vision of the world we want. We truly do think as one in our outer creations. Some people have more influence over this outer world than others. This is demonstrated by forms of media that reach large audiences. Vision is also influenced by people in power who persuade large groups of people to do their bidding. High positions in government and large corporations are some examples. These people are not the true creators in your world.

The most influential thoughts are highly-focused thoughts of manifestation. This is why it is important to remain centered, with desire and expectation, if you want to be a creator in your world. Most people do not stay focused in their creative desires. They float from one thought form to another as if they were observing a movie. With pure intention and focused thought, you add prana, or God force, to that thought. As more prana is added to that thought, it gains energy and light. This stronger light then attracts others to it. As more and more people attune to this thought, it goes through a transformation of manifestation. This happens on the inner planes. You see the results of manifested thoughts in the physical world.

This is what is happening in your world today. Those enlightened souls who desire a world of love and peace are the world's true creators. They are the ones who are holding the focus of your future world. Their thoughts and intentions are already coming into form. Your world is evolving because of these enlightened souls who are currently on earth. Add your own highest intentions and thoughts for this place and you will manifest a world of love and peace.

You are your thoughts. You are creators. Do we add to the creation of what we truly desire for others and ourselves, or not? This is something we each must answer. Hold the focus of a world of love and peace and that will become your reality. It is the desire of this planet at this time. It is your future.

In a state of joy, this is all of your heart's intention.

April 18, 2005

Flow with the Rhythm of Life

Timing is everything. Life is on purpose. There is a grand plan, and everything is orchestrated to flow in rhythm and in harmony. The key to purposeful living is to know this flow and to flow with it. Ride the rhythm of life.

There are universes within universes. Even though they appear separate, they actually breathe as one. You know you are in the flow when you feel the pulse of the universe. In sync, your pulse mirrors it. There are no coincidences, just rhythms of life breathing as One.

All of life is a dance. This is called 'living the joy of life.' Truly, life is joy, and joy is life. The melodies of life are the emotions and feelings that pulsate in rhythm frequencies. Emotions and feelings give movement to this rhythm. All emotions and feelings are good. Their range gives the rhythm and the undulating movement of life. Acknowledge all emotions and feelings and let them pass through you.

Then let them go. If you try to hang on to them, you are restricting their natural flow. Restriction and constriction get you out of sync with the pulse of the universe. It is like trying to hold back a river from rushing over the falls. Gravity pulls it down. When left unobstructed, the water flows effortlessly down the path in its own special dance of life. Imagine yourself as this flowing river. Go with the flow and enjoy the journey. As you bump up against life's rocks, embrace them and they will then let you slide by. Fear and judgment will send you into an ever-circulating whirlpool until you relax and go with the flow again.

The phrase, 'Let go and let God' has relevance. The wholeness of God, or Source, does have a grand plan. Trust. Source is all-encompassing, all-knowing. Our greatest mission, and reward, is to stay in that flow of life. We are intricately woven into the whole of creation. Honor your place in creation that flows in and around you. You are life itself.

This is the heartbeat of God.

April 24, 2005

Internal Message I

It is I, Jesus the Christ, who comes to you to say that at all times we are One. And in that Oneness, we are all masters. You can claim your mastery in this lifetime. It is a personal choice for each. Regardless of your decision, you are still masters in the sense that divinity of the creative God is within you and everyone at all times. There have been masters on the earth who have been aware of their mastery.

This is a unique time. Since all of humanity has various aspects of the one God, each person will contain a different aspect of that mastery. As Buddha was an enlightened Master, he knew that and proclaimed it. You can too. To be a true master, you need to see yourself within every person and life form. Yes, everything in consciousness is a life form. Air and the elements, such as the mineral kingdom, are included.

This is the time of great change. The change is more from within than without. The inner changes need to come before the outer changes. When you truly love unconditionally, you will be unaffected by the thoughts and opinions of others. You will embrace love and a connection with all of life. Without accepting this love, you will, unfortunately, let it pass as a ship would unknowingly pass an island in the dark.

Peace within one's self is what allows you to open to the Christ Energy within you. Unless the Christ Energy drives your changes, the outer world will not be affected. You can be the calm of the sea or the eye of the tornado. This right use of power is the mastery of a divine and creative being. This power is not only from within, but also from a collective God energy. The Collective Whole contains all knowledge, wisdom, love and light.

In the years ahead, you will experience many storms in your physical realm. Points of calm, known as 'lighthouses,' will reside in many people. You will know others with this 'lighthouse' energy; and in this knowing, there will be bliss, love, and inter-dimensional connection. You will be able to connect with all realms through understanding.

The changes on this earth are purposeful. There is a flow to the energy with these changes. All of you think as individuals now, but you are more connected at a higher level than you may realize. There are no coincidences and there are no separations. No need to force things to happen. Everything will unfold naturally. Follow your intuition—follow all aspects to the One consciousness. Allow this to flow with ease. This life is meant to be one of ease and joy. It will be, if you so choose.

Wake up to your full awareness and see your connections. This leads to mastery of your being on all levels of understanding. You will be able to do as Jesus the Christ, for I am you and you are me. You need not look up to me. We are brothers and sisters in the Divinity of the One Love. Be the peace that you are. Be the masters that you are. Truly be the masters that you are.

I am the 'Love of the Heart.'
I am the 'Love of the Heart.'
I am the 'Love of the Heart.'

August 21, 2005

Internal Message II

It is I, Jesus the Christ, that comes to you this day. It is I, 'The Love of the Heart.' The heart: we all are one and truly that heart does beat as One. There is only One of you here on the earth in full realization. There are many parts, acting in individual ways, but this is not as it appears. There is One of you living out this life on earth.

What has happened in your country most recently has impacted everyone around the world. Truly, times are changing. You are waking up to the true reality of being a multi-soul being. The devastation that you see is just one part of the whole crying out for help. It is wise for everyone to respond. Other countries should be given the opportunity to respond and your country to receive. You see, you are part of an awakening reality that one cannot do anything without affecting all life forms—even beyond humanity.

These types of events will continue to occur until the whole wakes up. This does not mean every individual; but rather the total consciousness of humanity. How long that will take is up to you. As individuals, the greatest thing that you can do to accelerate consciousness is to send the highest intentions of prayer thoughts out to the world.

Each individual, as well as any organization, can direct the flow of energy where it is most needed. The pulse and nerve centers rely on individuals' right intentions, thoughts and prayers rather than deeming it the responsibility of government or other organizations. Without individual focus, the other forms of service and communication will progress poorly or not at all.

People ask what can be done. You can do a lot right where you are. With full intention, send Light to all individuals in need. You will be doing more than you realize.

Yes, there will be a time when all of humanity will work together for the good of the universe. Your media does not reveal how this is happening now, yet there are many examples of this change. If it were not for the intention of individuals, advanced technology in communication would not be fully effective. With each natural catastrophe, you will see this awareness go deeper and wider. Response will increase with quicker results and less devastation to the psyche of the souls affected by an event. It is individual efforts that will change the whole, including governments and organizations.

Just as each individual is connected to another in this life, you are also connected inter-dimensionally. You are assisted by others in other dimensions. This will become more evident as time moves forward. You will see many changes on your earth that could not, would not, occur otherwise. It is important to keep an open mind. (Larry feels and shows great emotion now.)

You are all so dearly loved. If you could realize this, you would be in a state of bliss. Just know that all of you are supported in many ways, now and in the times ahead. Everything that occurs in your world is on purpose and contributes to the good of the whole. Rest assured that all is well, and you are loved. Go in peace each day and be the peace that the world needs.

This is the 'Love of the Heart.'
This is the 'Love of the Heart.'
This is the 'Love of the Heart.'

Larry's postscript: This was a very emotional connection for me because I was able to feel so much love and support coming through to me. Much came to me that can't be expressed in words. Iamaste.

September 4, 2005

Internal Message III

It is I, Jesus the Christ who comes to you this day — and everyday. The time in which you are living is unique. And yet, it is like every other day. Each of you is also unique, and yet you are all alike for you are One and the same. It is the big dichotomy that you face in the years ahead. Express your uniqueness and your individuality. Truly become aware of the realization of that inter-connection between all and everything.

I can give you some advice that will make this easier. Operate out of the awareness of love. Have the awareness that each and every one of you is love and an expression of love. By expressing that love that you are, you are also reflecting that love of others. As you reflect love you also express the unique aspect of divinity. Just as a diamond has many facets that reflect the light, each facet is part of the whole. Together it becomes one bright light. Without each facet, that brightness would not be as strong or brilliant.

The whole of earth's humanity is to reflect the full, dynamic expression of that divinity, that Godhead, which is now present. By operating out of love, you are not a part of the inconsistencies and any expressions of those who do not reflect light. Focus on the light, rather than on the darkness behind it.

If you focus on the light of your brothers and sisters, you will not see the shadow side that they also harbor. The shadow side is a part of all as well. This shadow side is an expression of duality in this physical realm. Understanding the expression of who you are means fully experiencing yourself in opposite terms.

The physical realm is about the duality of opposites. There is really no good or bad involved in this. It is all expressions of the whole. Just as you see earth change and people react quite differently to those changes (most recently, those caused by Hurricane Katrina)*, you view the best and worst of people. Without this full expression, you would not completely appreciate the wholeness of the experience. Do not judge those who have done things that you would have considered bad any more than you would honor those doing good. It is just a reflection of duality.*

Those aspects are only a part of what is real. You are much more than this body and this lifetime while you are on earth. You are much more—you are an aspect of divinity. Many believe that the role you play on earth is the greater part of who you are, but this is not true. It is only one aspect of your fullness. You live through all times and you exist multi-dimensionally. What you do on earth does affect all other aspects of yourself— your greater self.

Yes, it is important what you do with your life in this lifetime. Because you live through all times and dimensions, you have many opportunities to grow and expand—regardless of taking that opportunity or not. Since you are all different facets of this diamond, yet you are within the whole diamond, you will have many opportunities to express and reflect that light which you are.

In one sense, it really doesn't matter if you take full advantage of this lifetime or not. Still, know it has great impact if you do. This in itself is a dichotomy that is difficult to understand in your current physical form. You are love. When you focus on love, you cannot go wrong, as you would say.

There are many concerns at this time—many viewpoints and approaches about the direction of earth and the consequences of it. It's not about what another being or entity is doing. It's about you, and what you are doing and choose to do in the future.

You see, in one sense of the word, you are a reflection of the whole. You do reflect the whole. It may seem as if a lot of responsibility is being put upon you. Know that you are supported in many ways that you may not fully understand. Yes, you do have great responsibility, but you also have immense support and you cannot help but succeed in those responsibilities.

One innate ability that you have is to draw upon the support offered. It comes in many forms and from many realms. With your right intention, the heavens are at your beaconing. The angelic kingdom, as well as those from your past and your future, is at your beckoning. Yes, you can call upon the support of ones who have lived many lifetimes ago or you can call upon the support of ones who will live in the future. You are much more than what you believe you are: You are the past; you are the present; you are the future. Since you are that, you are automatically connected to all by your intention.

Not limited by distance and time, intentions are powerful. They are instantaneous. Yes, I do say that you have the support of all that is because you are all that is. Be in peace with all that you are because you are pure love. Be in a state of joy that is your true awareness. Love and joy are your true heritage and your true future. I am One with you and in you.

I am the 'Love of the Heart.'
I am the 'Love of the Heart.'
I am the 'Love of the Heart.'

September 18, 2005

We are Coming Together

It is I, Jesus the Christ, that comes to you this day. It is I, the 'Love of the Heart.' The heart: we all have one and truly that heart does beat as One. There is only one of you in full realization on earth. There are many parts, acting in individual ways, but this is not as it appears. There is one of you living out this life on earth.

Recent events: *What has happened in your country most recently has impacted everyone around the world (as there is only one of us here). Truly times are changing. You are waking up to the truth of individuals containing multiple realities. The devastation that you see is just one part of the whole crying out for help. It is wise for everyone to respond. Other countries should be given the opportunity to respond while the United States receives.*

You are part of an awakening reality where your responses will affect all life forms—even those beyond humanity. Events with the purpose of awakening will continue to occur until the whole wakes up. This does not mean every individual, but rather the total consciousness of humanity. How long that will take is up to you. The greatest thing that individuals can do to hasten the awakening process is to send prayer thoughts out to the world through the highest of intentions. Each individual, as well as any organization, can take part in directing the flow of energy where it is most needed.

Within government and organizations, the pulse and nerve centers do not lie. It is the right intention, thoughts and prayers that each person offers that make a difference. For without these, other forms of service and communication will slow or not progress well.

People ask what can be done. Tell them that they can do a great deal right where they are. They can start by sending light to those individuals in all areas of need. This is especially advantageous when done with full intention. Yes, there will be a time when all humanity will work together for the good of the universe.

Although your media does not show evidence of a broadening awareness, there are many examples of working together. If it were not for the intention of individuals, advanced technology in communication would not be fully effective. A deeper and wider awareness will accompany each natural catastrophe. Responses will increase with quickening results and less damage to the soul.

It is individual efforts that will change the whole rather than large organizations and government entities. Just as you are connected to another in this life, you are also connected interdimensionally. You are assisted by others in new dimensions.

This will become more evident with time. You will see many changes that could not (would not) occur otherwise. It is important to keep an open mind. (Larry feels and shows great emotion now).

You are all so dearly loved. If you could know this, you would be in a state of bliss. Just know you are all supported in many ways now and in the times ahead. Everything that occurs in your world is deliberate and has a purpose for the good of the whole. Rest assured that all is well and you are loved. Go in peace each day and be the peace that the world needs at this time.

This is the 'Love of the Heart.'
This is the 'Love of the Heart.'
This is the 'Love of the Heart.'

Larry's note: This was a very emotional connection for me because I was able to feel so much love and support. Much came to me that can't be expressed in words. Iamaste.

October 4, 2005

Take Your Focus Away from the Storm

It is I, Jesus the Christ, that comes to you this day. Feel my connection with you. We are always connected. Stay out of fear. You are always connected to me. This is a time of great change. Feel this change. You are a part of Gaia.

It is a time of repositioning and awakening. When you awaken, you are not as before. This is what is happening to Mother Earth, and there are many natural changes as repositioning occurs. Truly humanity has a part in this. There is cooperation which is needed for the times ahead. We are all awakening and repositioning. Humanity will naturally do what is best for Mother Earth; in turn, this will be best for Humanity.

There is a storm and upheaval upon the earth. Where do you wish to be? Do you wish to be in the middle of the storm or rise above the storm? That choice is yours. You are empowered to be where you want to be. In order to rise above the storm, just take your focus away from the center of the storm and become the observer.

It is through the awakening process that you become more of the observer. Upon awakening, you realize that you are not your body. You are a spiritual being; you are energy called 'love.' Love is what we all are. Everything is love in its pure essence. Focus on the love that you are and you will rise above the storm, a position that will be most helpful.

What is coming is the interconnectedness of all things. Harmony, peace, and creativity, unknown for a long time, will come to humanity. You must first overcome your insecurities and know your capacity with full awakening. Just become aware that you are all-powerful and you are interconnected with all that is. Until you come to that point of awareness, it will be difficult to overcome your fears and stay out of the storm. The fear of separation keeps you in the storm of this transition period. There is no right or wrong about where you are in this process, since all play a role.

Some of you will need a clear head and clear thinking to understand and give clear answers. There will be answers to the challenges in the months and years ahead. Do not interpret this to be a time of retribution for things done or not done. It is just a natural, awakening process of Gaia's energy to ascend to her new position in the Cosmos.

As a part of Mother Earth, you are a part of this awakening because of your interconnectedness. As all rise, the storms will dissipate. Vibrations will be totally different.

At this time, does 'the one called Nita' have any questions?

Nita: Is ascension the evolution of earth's changes or the evolution of our changes?

Answer: *Each affects the other. Humanity and Mother Earth needed to awaken to the loving presence of the Source. It is appropriate for this vibration and transformation to occur. Humanity, each and collectively, has made this decision. It is a collective decision among all energy sources.*

Nita: In what ways are the vibrations that are occurring now, on many energy fields, affecting us?

Answer: *How this energy is felt varies from individual to individual. It all depends on the vibration that the individual carries at the time the energy intercepts the individual. One person may have headaches and another will have other symptoms. It will vary. In the years ahead, energy disruptions will not be the same as now.*

Nita: What information does Larry need to know about his back, vertebras, and pain he is experiencing?

Answer: *The one called Larry needs to know that he is in control of his own body. Yet, on a physical level, there is much more that is going on than he knows. This is why he is frustrated in seeing no changes in his back condition. He does not see all that is multi-dimensional. At this time, there are many things occurring concerning his physical changes. If he only knew how broad his work is, and how much awareness he is to bring to this earth, he would be pleased with his physical endurance.*

Energetically, there is a great exchange going on, straining his body's structural system. My advice to him is to stay above the storm. He knows what it is like above the storm. At a higher level, he will be able to absorb the energies to gain structural support. People in his life will continue to be a support for him. In the years ahead, all will see how they support each other in the whole. Larry remembers Home. I am only a thought away and in each and every one of you. You are loved.

This is the 'Love of the Heart.'
This is the 'Love of the Heart.'
This is the 'Love of the Heart.'

October 9, 2005

Peace

Peace. Peace to you. Peace carries a vibration—a vibration that brings peace. And peace is the core of who you are. Peace is at that center of silence—a center of Source of all that is and of all that will be. Know that you are also of the Source. When you are at peace with yourself, all things are possible.

Creation comes from a place of peace. You are entering a period in your calendar year that some of you call Christmas. The message of peace is what Christmas brings for many. Yet how many of you are really at peace right now? Unfortunately, most of you are not. It is within you to be at peace, so that you can create and share peace with others.

You ask about how to create peace within yourself. You know that you are of God, and that everything exists in the eternal now. Truly take in these words. You are God. The term 'you' refers to all of life, all of creation, all of 'I Am.' Although there are many labels referring to the great 'I Am,' each one means 'God.'

In the center of God is love. In the human realm, the center of love is the heart. And so I speak from the 'Love of the Heart.' Be peace. Be the peace the world is seeking, and your world will be transformed. For those who read or hear these words, it is you who is creating them.

Now you may ask about how to create peace for others. You can share peace by presenting a vibration to others. Just be peace. It is not necessary to say anything. Peace will be absorbed by others. In itself, this will create the necessary atmosphere.

Since it is Christmas, you may ask about the greatest gift that you can give to your loved ones. It is your peace. When you are truly at peace with yourself, you are in a state of love—a state of joy—a state of perfection and can share this spirit with others.

Humanity has created a great illusion. That illusion is separateness. Truly it does not exist, yet you see and experience it everywhere. Feel the connection with others this Christmas season. Share your peace with them. They will feel the 'I Am' within themselves. Realizing their joy and peace as it permeates their bodies, they will share it through their thoughts and actions.

When you give of yourself, you are truly giving to yourself. This is why the act of giving can bring great joy to everyone. For in the giving and receiving, you truly awaken to the Oneness that you are. When giving comes from the heart, the recipient feels that vibration. In return, it is mirrored back to the one who gives.

It is important to find that peace within yourself to navigate the times ahead. For when you are at peace, you are in the flow of the universe. You are in the flow of God. In your world, regardless of what may appear on the outside, all will be well within your inner self. Now all the power of the universe is within you and within your grasp. Using this knowledge, you can focus, create, and manifest peace within the universe.

What do you want to create during this Christmas season and in the years ahead? Peace...or that which is not of peace? The choice is yours. You are the creators. You are the creation. As creators, all things are possible. You write your future. No one is pre-destined (How could that be when you are the 'Gods' doing the creating?).

The quickest way to find peace within yourself is to be the peace that you give to others. All religions and philosophies speak of The Golden Rule. It is the ultimate truth of peace: Give unto others as you wish to receive.

You seek to be loved and to love. You seek to be in a state of joy and to give joy—unconditionally. You seek to feel connected and to connect with others. You seek internal harmony and harmony with others. You seek to be in a state of health and well being. You seek to be of God and to see God within others. You seek to come Home to your Source and, yet, are the Source of Home for others. And so it is; and so it is; and so it is.

This is the 'Love of the Heart.'
This is the 'Love of the Heart.'
This is the 'Love of the Heart.'

December 4, 2005

Playing the Game

Source: You all come from Source. Time is not what you perceive it to be. Your bodies are catching up to higher consciousness. Your consciousness is no longer where it was. Your bodies are connected to Source and you will respond, as you need to respond. You will experience certain medical scenarios that are needed in this physical world, yet remember you are not truly of this physical world. Be at peace.

How do you incorporate many realities into one? That is what you are being asked to do. Incorporating many realities into one is done by intention, and so your intention is all-important.

What drives your intention, desire, passion, and purpose for many of you is to create that which you already know. You know it deep within you, as your connection to Source. You are here to bring that greater awareness to earth, a purpose similar to many other Light Workers.

Each of you is a part of the whole — the sum of the whole. Each person has a different purpose or mission. And, with that comes a different focus or desire. This is why it is so important to find your passion because when you find it, you know you are following your mission.

Originally, all of you started out as separate beings, each with an individual focus. This is as it should be. Yet that time is changing, for you are starting to see that your missions are interwoven.

Right now, there is only one game on earth. It is the awakening of the whole. You are each a part of that game. There are many groups forming on earth. Groups come together because they have something in common. They are drawn together like magnets. The individuals' energy is the attraction. If you are involved with many groups, it is because each group plays a certain role within the Divine Plan.

As time goes on, groups will serve an even more important role, as individuals will experience the energy of that group. As each group activates this energy, it will expand, becoming a part of other groups. This process will continue as part of the game plan. It will continue until each of you remembers who you really are. Remembering your Source is what will transform earth.

Your physical manifestation is a result of a certain time period. So much is happening at other, deeper levels within individuals and within groups. If you are aware, you are able to see this happening now. At some point in time, the plan will fully unfold, and there will be rapid change.

What is your role now? What should you really be doing with your energy or focus? The answer lies within. Each soul has a slightly different mission. Become quiet and listen to Source within you, for Source is always available to you. You are always connected. It is important to take time in your life to separate yourself from the activities of the day so you can renew with Source.

Soon you will become more conscious of that connection on a moment-to-moment basis. When you can connect with

Source at all times, you will be living on purpose and will find peace within yourself and all others.

Truly, Source has set up a game for you. You just don't fully realize that you are a co-creator with Source. Without your connection to Source and the larger overview, how could you fully appreciate and enjoy the game?

With rapid speed, you are beginning to realize that this part of the game is coming to an end. You are becoming more aware of the larger game plan. You are co-creating this moment in evolution with Source. 'You' means the 'collective you.' When this game ends, the 'collective you' will create another version of the same game.

What is the purpose of all of this? It is to know and experience the collective whole for yourself. Source, or God energy, is understood through experiences. Source is all-expansive. The totality of Source is beyond comprehension of the individual soul's awareness, yet this imprint has been placed in our cellular memory. It is difficult to understand this dichotomy until you have reached certain levels of awareness.

You are at the final leg of this game. You will see the result. Some of you will glimpse the finish line. It has been a great game. Awakening allows you to fully enjoy the excitement of the game. Time appears longer so you can experience the joy of awakening and the thrill of the experience that you have completed.

This is done by collapsing time. This means that you become aware of all time. What this does is broaden and enhance *your experiences, much more so than what you perceived while in human form. The game is multi-experienced and multidimensional. It exists beyond linear reality. As the game continues, it will bring together all of the different experiences of past, present, and future. This, in itself, brings the collective whole to a higher level.*

The game has many life forms as players — many life forms beyond your world. They will enter your game as you become aware of their presence, even though they have always been there with you. Source is so expansive that how could it be otherwise?

As you get closer to the end of the game, you will feel your expanded connection to Source. Your awareness will continue to expand. Remember throughout this time that everything is of Source. With that awareness, comes the realization that everything is connecting.

Everyone and everything affects the whole. You cannot even blink your eye without affecting the furthest reaches of the universe. This is so. This is because you are a part of the energy called Source. It is not something that can be put into words. It could be called Light or Love, yet this does not even begin to describe what Source is.

You are at the end of this game. Celebrate it by awakening to who you really are. Your awakening, just as for all the souls that are awakening, is the exciting part of this juncture in time and space. This is Source.

February 5, 2006

Personal note: At the beginning of the transmission, when the message referred to the body, I felt rapid heart palpitations. This physical experience was similar to the symptoms I had over a week ago, before I went on prescribed medication. I hadn't experienced any of the original symptoms since I went on the medication.

I believe the recurrence of the palpitations is a special message to me that my body symptoms are more than a medical issue. I find this interesting since the sensations occurred when the message implied that the body was not in sync with the higher consciousness.

Collection 6

WHAT IF...Series

WHAT IF...Series

By the year 2006, I arrived at a stage where I felt it was time to act on the insights and wisdom I had gained over the years. Books and workshops were secondary in my life as I became aware of how we can visualize and create the world we desire. First, we need to have a clear vision. The result of this visioning is contained in my "What If ... Series." This collection weaves my experiences and insights into provoking thoughts for you to ponder.

WHAT IF...
We had the attitude that we already have received what we desire?

What if we had the attitude that we already have received what we desire? With this attitude, I believe we would accomplish much more than we do. We would manifest much more in our lives. The key is to skip the "trying" and "wishing" for something. Trying rarely gets us anything but more trying. Wishing is a projection into the future, and we really have only the present moment.

"Fake it 'til you make it" is a phrase that we have all heard. To me, this phrase means when we presume something long enough, we will bring it into our lives. We are also saying that what we want or desire is already ours, regardless of whether someone else believes it. As long as we truly believe it or know it is possible, it is so. The way to know something is possible is to keep presuming, or acting, as if it *is possible*. The more we presume that something is already part of our lives, the more power it has to manifest.

Relying on this presuming attitude for many years now, I have practiced it often while creating ongoing experiences of Oneness with all of life. It has been my good fortune to have memories of Oneness experiences while in other states of consciousness. Even when the world around me doesn't express Oneness, I still presume that we are all One.

As the years go by, more and more loving people have entered my life. In more recent years, I've had conscious experiences of merging into Oneness. My presumption has created more and more of the Oneness that I've desired.

At some point we no longer have to presume. That which we had presumed will become constant in our lives. We are the creators of our lives. When we focus with conviction on what we desire, we presume that we have it. And, we do.

January 22, 2006

WHAT IF...
We relied and acted on personal intuition?

What if we relied and acted on personal intuition? I believe we would make greater strides in creating a loving, interconnected world. We would be less fearful of our intuition-based decisions if we truly knew the source of this inner voice. I believe our intuition is that one connecting link we all have with our God/Source and our high self. Intuitive decisions serve the good of the whole rather than individual benefit. When we make a decision based on our intuition, we are making that decision from a greater informational source than just our individual knowledge and physical awareness. That informational source is the collective of all souls, our high self, and all that we call God/Source.

The way most people describe their intuition is calling it a "gut feeling." It is a deep inner feeling, or knowing, that speaks to us from our core. Unlike wishful thinking, intuitional messages are not always fully understood. In fact, intuitional messages may even *go against* our rational thinking. For this reason alone, many people do not act on their intuitions. An intuitive message is based on what is best for all concerned. As physical beings, we do not cognitively see the situation from this higher, more inclusive perspective. This is where we learn to trust. The more we use our intuition, the more we realize that we can trust it. We gain clarity, and comfort. We learn to rely on intuition as a "greater knowing" that is looking out not only for the individual, but for the good of the whole.

Over the years, I have come to rely on my intuition as my best friend. This doesn't mean that I have always understood, nor felt comfortable with, what has been asked of me. I have always felt good, however, about following my intuitive decisions, remembering that reasons for intuitive actions aren't always revealed.

Many times I've questioned my inner voice. Is that inner voice truly my intuition, or is it just wishful thinking? If I genuinely question it, I may not act on the message for some time. If the inner voice *is* my intuition, it will keep annoying me until I do act on it. After a while, I can determine the difference and am more willing to act quickly on those intuitive messages. This recognition allows me to accomplish more.

By using the interconnecting link we call intuition, we can more easily accomplish our goals. Our intuition becomes a trusted friend. When we use our intuition in conjunction with our other God-given gifts, we create a better world.

January 28, 2006

WHAT IF...
We realized that life isn't survival of the fittest?

What if we realized that life isn't survival of the fittest? Rather, life is the constant giving and receiving of love. We have been programmed to believe that all living things are struggling to survive. This is accomplished by competing for a limited supply of what we want or need to survive. In this scenario the strongest or smartest life form, competes with its opponent for the limited resources that it needs to survive. Maybe there is a higher conscious decision at work here.

Case in point: Several months ago while I was driving to work through a residential area, I experienced a life-altering occurrence. Many shrubs and trees formed a canopy over the road. I stepped out of time and saw myself merge with these life forms. In this state, I saw the shrubs and trees grow from small forms to their majestic, mature life forms. There was no competition for the sunlight or growing space, but rather conscious individual and collective decisions made out of love, deciding which branch and leaf would continue to grow and which ones would not. These decisions were made for the collective good of the shrubs and trees, ensuring survival.

This held true within the same life form as well as within different species of plants. Since I was as one with these plants, I felt their ongoing communication among all life forms. I noticed no feelings of struggle or anger among the different life forms. On the contrary, there was a strong feeling of cooperation and love. It was the best decision for the good of the whole. At a higher level of consciousness, even these life forms knew their Oneness. At their level of consciousness, all were aware of the whole—just as I was in those moments. I observed a dance of life. It was a harmonious expression of give and take.

If plants can have this level of cooperation, why is it so hard for humanity? Tears come as I ponder that. I see so much potential in humanity. We are a species that has the co-creative powers of God. Imagine our potential. As a human race, when we decide to work together in coopera-tion and love, we will transform earth. We will transform all that is. Our world is awakening. We will create heaven on earth through our choices. We can project a harmoni-ous world.

November 10, 2006

WHAT IF...
We became conscious, multidimensional spiritual beings?

What if we became conscious, multidimensional spiritual beings? What would that look like? It might mean that we could consciously leave one reality to experience other realities. For most of us, becoming a conscious, multidimensional being has more to do with expanding our conscious awareness in this world. With increased conscious awareness, we move from *thinking* we are all One to *knowing* that we are all One.

When that magical change takes place, we start to pay more attention to our intuition. That intuition, which is in each of us, is the electrical circuit which connects us to our greater whole. Think of it this way: We are light bulbs that have electrical wires connecting to an electrical power source, (God). Each light bulb receives its electrical current from the same power source. As multidimensional beings, we lose that focus of the "Small I" and begin to operate from the "Big I." We realize that everything the "Small I" does affects the "Big I." Giving and receiving is one and the same, and lack does not exist. The "Big I" contains all that is. It is all a flow of energy—a flow of love. With that knowing comes the desire to be of service to the "Big I." Without fear of lack, nothing derails us. Energy flows abundantly.

We become excited and joyful in the game of life. Our repressed creative spirit returns. As we support each other, others support us. With heightened awareness, we are more in tune to the needs of others. We do not even consider what we will receive in return. We are giving to ourselves. It is a direct knowing that as One, all is being taken care of. We experience a creative life rather than a life of struggle. Life expands in all directions. As we operate as One, our powers increase. Our knowledge and wisdom increase. We become conscious, multidimensional spiritual beings.

As such, we move out of the limiting beliefs of the three-dimensional world. We use information from our past, present, and future lives to support ourselves in the only time we have. This time is the present moment. We are then able to step out of space and time to see a greater expansion of who we are. We move from a limiting three-dimensional consciousness to a limitless multidimensional consciousness. An entirely new and expansive world will be available to us. Think about this. Consider the difference between a 110-volt outlet and a 220-volt outlet. Connecting with a 220-volt outlet, our light would extend much further into the night sky (awareness).

Our time of awakening is here at hand. It is now time to step outside of our self-created cell, and awaken to our full potential as sparks of God. Some of us are awakening now, and others will awaken soon. This awakening is for us. All "Small I's" are a part of the "Big I." Let's enjoy the journey of awakening as we become conscious, multidimensional spiritual beings.

November 13, 2006

WHAT IF...
We lived life from our authentic selves?

What if we lived life from our authentic selves? What would that look like? We would move out of a world of illusions and into a world of authentic reality. The first step is to learn to know ourselves. We allow that knowing when we are willing to see ourselves clearly. What does that mean? Perhaps we are perfect spiritual beings having a human experience. Could it be that we already have everything inside of us that we need?

Let's see ourselves clearly. We are beings creating different life experiences for our soul's growth. What if there were no right or wrong, nor good or bad? What if there were merely opposites in a world of duality? Suppose we knew that we were sparks of God and "all that is" already exists within? All powers and abilities are then available to us. We would no longer ask for approval from others, as we would innately have the approval and self-worth we were seeking.

Having a false understanding of ourselves creates the need for others' approval. As long as we have this need, it is difficult to be our full authentic selves. When we seek others' approval, we sacrifice our freedom to be authentic. Energy that could be used to express our uniqueness and divinity is instead used to create illusions and delusions.

How do we act from our authentic selves? First, we should desire to be authentic. Next, we need to identify the obstacles that keep us from being authentic. These may include various people, old habits, or old belief systems. As we become more aware of these obstacles, we change anything that keeps us from reaching our goal. As humans we are interdependent. We can seek others who support us as we live from our authentic selves. We can fill any voids with new, supportive friends, new habits and new belief systems. As we live in the present, it is easier to live as authentic beings.

Now we are free to focus our creative energies toward truly meaningful endeavors. We can live our lives through our creative passions. Sincerely appreciating each other, we will see the uniqueness, the divinity, and the love within each authentic person. Authenticity will allow us to experience that Oneness we have with each other and with all other life forms. When we are authentic, we let our lights shine. We are wondrous beings of love.

November 17, 2006

WHAT IF...
Our eyes were the gateway to our souls?

What if our eyes were the gateway to our souls? When we look into another person's eyes during a heart opening, it is possible to look into that person's soul. The eyes are a magical gateway. They know no limitations as they penetrate through all dimensions. The heart is the key to that gateway. We need to take time to open our hearts as we peer into the eyes of another's soul.

As we look into another's eyes, we are able to see others as they really are. Space and time drop away as our energy merges with theirs. We truly do become One in that moment. All masks and pretense fall away. We become serene and joyful because there is nothing to fear. In that merger, we see ourselves in that other person. There is no real difference—only the outward creations of each soul. Other souls carry the same emotions that our souls carry. The desires of their souls match ours. Both of us have a desire to return Home to the Oneness of God/Source. Their souls seek the same joy, happiness, and love. All things that are permanent within us are also permanent within them. We are both timeless and creative beings, taking a moment in time to exchange divinity.

Divinity has no separation—just different forms of self-expression. All dimensions are playgrounds of creation. When we are able to see ourselves in others, we are then able to expand our awareness and life experiences. The experiences of others enter into our own awareness. We are able to see all aspects of creation which helps us to become multidimensional. As multidimensional beings, we are aware of our expanded selves. This expanded self includes the recognition of our connection with all souls. As individual souls, we may have chosen to forget that connection. It is time to reawaken and come back into that collective knowing.

When we take time to open our hearts and look into the eyes of another, we will actually be looking at ourselves. Our world will expand instantly, and we will have a key to coming Home.

November 22, 2006

WHAT IF...
We really felt good about ourselves?

What if we really felt good about ourselves? The world would be totally different. We would see a world where our interactions with others would be inclusive, rather than exclusive. We would celebrate our self-worth and the worth of others. We would take pride in ourselves, in our families and friends, and in our communities. All of our resources and energy would build a better world for all. It begins with our children. How we feel about others and ourselves is a result of our upbringing and the influences in our lives.

We live in a self-contained world. Our thoughts and feelings affect everyone else on this planet. Energy can be positive or negative; if it is negative, it becomes destructive. When we do not feel good about ourselves, we feel a need to bring down others—to make us look superior. Our need to feel superior is directly proportionate to the extent of our feelings of unworthiness.

This destructive energy causes all kinds of negative results, personally and globally. Negative feelings can lower our immune systems. Many forms of sickness are an indirect result of a low immune system. Our state of mind affects productivity in the work force and in our personal lives. Low self-worth can cause tempers to flare and prejudices to surface. When this negative state of mind gains collective energy, it can even lead to war.

We can make a difference. We can trust in and accept our own self-worth. By living a life that expresses self-worth and believing that the truth of goodness is in all people, we change the world. As parents and grandparents, we have the most impact on our children when we show them their inherent value, by being and expressing love. Love expressed gives value and self-worth to all that it touches. When a person experiences love, in any of its forms, self-worth increases. The more love and confidence that we extend to humanity's consciousness, the easier it is for others to recognize their self-worth.

As a collective of humanity, we will become One when we accept that each of us has worth and value—regardless of race, creed, age, gender, or any other perceived differences. We are worthy. We know we are forms of that unified love as we go on to express our unique qualities.

November 27, 2006

WHAT IF...
We believed imagination to be one of our greatest gifts?

What if we believed imagination to be one of our greatest gifts? How might we use it to our best advantage? It is important to realize that everything we create starts with a thought. Our imagination gives us seed materials for those thoughts. To create a new and better world for ourselves and others, we need imagination. Imagination feeds those creative thoughts.

Another way to look at this is that everything created starts with a thought. Emotions or feelings develop from these thoughts. Feelings give fluidity to creation. Without feelings, there is no desire; without desire, vibrations would stop. Vibrations are essential to life; therefore, we must have desire to have life. It all starts with our imagination.

New stimuli for our imagination come from many sources. While in human form, dreams and multidimensional experiences feed our creative thought processes. We learn to become more aware of those experiences. We take those visions of higher realities and anchor them to our consciousness. Focusing on those thoughts, we associate strong emotions and desire with them. The more emotion we add to those visions, the more we will accelerate the manifestation process.

Visions of heaven can be created on this earth—visions of world peace and harmony among all people and nations. We see visions of interconnection among all life forms. These visions are our reality of how interdependent and interconnected we really are.

We imagine a world where each person is open to another, a world where we all act in ways that are good for the whole. We can create anything we desire. Why not create a world in which fear is banished—a world in which wars and conflict do not exist. We can create a world where we put all of our energies into creative endeavors, accomplishing our efforts with love and divine realization. We imagine all things to be possible.

December 5, 2006

WHAT IF...
We were fully conscious of our greater selves?

What if we were fully conscious of our greater selves? What would that allow us to do? In human form while on earth, most of us believe we are just our physical bodies. Some of us are starting to be aware that we are more than just physical bodies—we have expanded selves. When we expand our consciousness, we are able to tap into past and future lives.

Outside of the third dimension, time and space become the eternal now. Many scientists believe that linear time is just a third-dimensional illusion. Many people believe we are evolving into the fifth dimension, which allows us to become more consciously expansive. Having greater awareness, fifth dimensional beings make the most of their whole being.

I believe that we have what some would consider past and future lives and that we can co-exist in many different dimensions. We are so much more than we have been led to believe. Since we are conscious of our human experience, we should take advantage of our expanded selves. When we become conscious of our larger soul selves, we are able to make better choices as humans.

While experiencing greater awareness, we are able to change our past as well as our future. A simple example would be how we change our past in history books. If we were to read about the Civil War in an American history book written in 2009, it would impact us differently from one written in 1909. As we learn and expand our understanding and knowledge of the past, we reshape our present understanding of our past, present, and future.

The choices we make in the present moment affect our past and our future. We may also learn consciously from our past lives. When we understand our past life experiences, we better understand why we have some of the phobias and behaviors in this lifetime. Healing those parts of us becomes easier. In the same way, if we go into our future, we can see where our present path is leading us. We can make changes that will give us a more promising future. Life becomes an experience of reaching our full potential.

Tapping into higher dimensional experiences also allows us to know our complete potential. When we learn to know who we are and reach our full potential, we will never return to being "just a physical body." We are fully empowered on all levels.

December 9, 2006

WHAT IF...
People loved each other unconditionally?

What if people loved each other unconditionally? How would we behave differently? We would live without fear of how others perceive us. We would experience acceptance without judgment. Without fear of ridicule or judgment, we would feel safe to express and be our true selves. We would be free to open up to others in ways that would show our deeper vision of who we are. We are all expressions of the Divine. We are looking for ways to share our unique gifts and talents with others. We have a unique perspective of life that no one else has. What we share with others enriches all of us. It is in this way that we come to know and feel our interconnection.

When we feel unconditional love from others, we want to respond in a similar way. The feeling of separation vanishes as we see the common ground in each other. We learn that we have similar desires, emotions, and needs. We begin to feel what others feel—their pain, their joy and their love.

It is at this point, we move from thinking only about ourselves to thinking about how all of our actions affect others. We are all interdependent and impact each other. Our desire then becomes one of wanting the best for all. We see that we are contributing to the good of the whole.

Only then do we feel intimate with each other. This

is where we are not afraid to show our deepest longings and expressions of who we are. It is in this personal expression that we feel our Oneness. We are expressions of unconditional love that is inherent in each of us.

In this state of unconditional love, we see each other as One. In this awareness, everyone is an extension of us. Intimacy is then something we have with everyone and with all of life. People will still play different roles in our lives, yet we will be intimate with all. Our true nature is that we are One. We have come Home to our true nature when we can fearlessly share intimate thoughts and unconditionally love all individuals.

December 14, 2006

WHAT IF...
We regarded all relationships as gifts?

What if we regarded all relationships as gifts? When we see our connections with others as gifts, it is easier to understand ourselves and to grow from the interactions within those connections. As One, we are mirrors for each other. Each person with whom we meet and interact, at some level, mirrors our image.

We see our physical self from many different perspectives. In relationships we may experience both positive and challenging interactions. Thoughts, emotions, feelings, and actions are expressed, so all relationships are instructive in that they allow us to grow and understand who we are. We have the choice to see ourselves from different perspectives.

If we are in relationships that are less than loving, we might not see ourselves as loving. The more we love ourselves, the more loving relationships we will have. One person may see someone as a quiet, smart, loving person, while someone else may see the same individual as arrogant, average, and detached. The qualities reflected are determined by individual filters and past experience.

The more emotionally charged our relationships are, the more we focus on those qualities being mirrored back to us. It may mean we need more development or growth in these areas. The *real* gift is that an opportunity emerges to change our perception of ourselves. We can struggle with our undesirable characteristics or we can become more tolerant.

In changing our perceptions, we have the potential to change our relationships. The more that we see ourselves as divine, loving reflections of God/Source, the more our relationships will reflect this. As we continue to grow, we will witness all relationships as they truly are, the loving reflections of all that is good and holy. We will begin to love all people as ourselves. All relationships will then mirror love. This is truly a gift.

December 22, 2006

WHAT IF...
We knew the power of a heart-felt hug?

What if we knew the power of a heart-felt hug? I believe we would give and receive more hugs. A magical thing happens during a hug. When two people come together in a hug, they are connecting energetically. For a moment, each person's essence merges, demonstrating a single recognition of both souls.

While in human form, we are able to experience energy in a very emotional way. Even angels are not able to experience a heart-felt hug as we humans can. Because of our intent to express love and connection with one another, we experience Oneness in a hug. When this happens, separation feelings dissipate.

Hugs overcome our feelings of being alone or separate. Through our imagination, we can recreate those emotions and feelings of a heart-felt hug. The cells of our body can't tell the difference between what actually physically happens to us and the actions we imagine in our minds. Since we are always recreating the eternal now, we can feel connected to others by regularly giving either physical or mental hugs.

Let's make a conscious decision to connect often with others. I recommend using a greeting that I believe originally came from Spirit. Then I put a little twist on it.

Used regularly, this greeting will create greater Oneness in the world. The greeting is Iamaste. This is my version of Namaste. Iamaste means "The love of God within me embraces the love of God within you. As such, we are One." Often I conclude written communication with this form of acknowledgement. My connection to and Oneness with others feels more real when I use this expression.

We have the power to feel the love of others. Expressing that love in the form of a heart-felt hug could be very emotional and rewarding and significantly contribute to our need for loving, physical contact. Let's take time to give others a heart-felt hug often.

Iamaste,
Larry

December 28, 2006

WHAT IF...
We allowed ourselves to be more vulnerable?

What if we allowed ourselves to be more vulnerable? We would find that we would feel liberated. Living life from a trusting perspective frees us to be ourselves. Allowing ourselves to be vulnerable can open us to criticism and hurt; however, the rewards may ultimately outweigh the risks involved.

When we allow ourselves to be vulnerable, we are saying that we trust the other person. We value the individual and want to get to know the person. It is one of the greatest gifts we can give to each other. This gift provides us with a clear lens to see into the soul of another. As we come to know others more deeply, we see how we are interconnected. There are no more pretenses. As we create authentic bonds, it becomes easier to live from our true selves.

By allowing ourselves to be vulnerable, we are admitting that there is nothing to fear. We recognize that each of us becomes transparent to another. As we speak our Truths, and live from authenticity, we become free. We no longer need to expend energy to protect a false image. We are now free to shine our light. Perceived weaknesses become our strengths. Our energy can now be used to heal illusions of separation.

In time, vulnerability fades from our thinking. We now see others as extensions of ourselves. We want the whole to know itself. By stepping into vulnerability, we overcome fear. All of us become fearless expressions of the whole.

We are Divine, conveying a brilliant kaleidoscope of self-expressions.

January 4, 2007

WHAT IF...
"The things that I do shall ye do also, and greater things than these shall ye do"?

What if the following statement by Jesus were true?

> "The things that I do shall ye do also, and greater things than these shall ye do."
> ~John 14:12 RSV

Jesus recognized that he was directly connected to Source. We are also coming to that same realization. Jesus was multidimensional in consciousness. If we are also multidimensional and realize our connection to Source, why can't we use those same powers reportedly used by Jesus? Many of us know that there are many levels of reality and states of consciousness.

One state is the dream state. When we are in a lucid dream state, we are conscious of our experiences and create them as we go. At will, we can manifest anything in this state. We can defy gravity, transport ourselves instantly, and change ourselves as we wish. It is believed that this state of consciousness is as real as our physical reality. When we are in this dream state, we vibrate at a different, higher frequency. Another vibration state is what is known as out-of-body experience. In this dimensional state we feel and experience life as fully conscious. In this dimension, we can walk through walls, travel through time, and manifest many things instantly. Maybe all we need to do is to know with 100% conviction, that we have that same Source power within ourselves while conscious in this dimension.

Jesus manifested things instantly. As we raise our vibration, our linear time also accelerates. Manifestation can speed up also. I understand that linear time acts as a safeguard to keep us from manifesting things we truly do not want. By giving ourselves time to reconsider our desires, we have been able to avoid a lot of undesirable creations. As we come into our own divine realization, we will no longer need a safeguard. We will be creating for the good of the whole, and will know that our thoughts and intentions create our reality.

What if "greater things than these shall ye do" comes about when we are directly supported by higher spiritual beings or "over lighted" by other avatars or other enlightened beings. Combined energy or support from other spiritual beings may allow us to do greater things than Jesus was able to do while on earth. There are many avatars that have supported humanity throughout time. Some of them are currently living on earth at this time: Sai Baba, Ammachi, Meyer Baba and Mother Meera. They are demonstrating similar things that Jesus was reported to have done.

Let's not limit our abilities. As we become more enlightened, answers and direction may become clearer to us. It is essential to join in consciousness with others of good intent. Our powers just may be multiplied to become the full creators that Source has intended for us.

January 9, 2007

WHAT IF...
We paid more attention to synchronicity in our lives?

What if we paid more attention to synchronicity in our lives? I believe we would see that synchronicity happens many times a day. With that awareness, we would begin to realize that we create those coincidences. We are the ones who ultimately bring events and people into our lives.

Coincidences are nothing more than the manifestation of our thoughts, intentions, and actions. The more that we understand and believe in this awareness, the more control and guiding ability we will have in our lives. When we allow the Universe to work for us, we save ourselves time and effort. This is often evident in simple ways such as finding something or arriving at an appointment on time.

When I was writing my last "What If," I wanted to use a quote from the Bible. I put great feeling into my intention of finding the exact passage easily. As I was reading an email article the next day, there was the precise passage, reference book, chapter, and verse. This approach saved me a lot of research time.

If I'm running late for work or a meeting, I will visualize the traffic lights turning green as I approach them. The more lead-time I can give the Universe to synchronize these events, the more likely the coincidence will take place. Coincidence enters our lives in many forms. Additional examples include when we think about someone we haven't talked to for a long time, and then they call, seemingly out of the blue. Another example is when we are looking for a parking space. We visualize a parking space becoming available. As luck would have it, someone vacates the very parking space on which we had focused. Many of these examples are simple. The intricacies of relationships, a more complex example of synchronicity, may take longer to manifest.

My first marriage did not produce the type of relationship I desired. By visualizing what I wanted my marriage to look like and by using deep intention and feeling, I declared my request. I did not tell the Universe how this relationship should materialize, only affirmed that it would. The Universe doesn't always create what is asked of it in the way we intend. However, given enough time, focus, and pure intent, eventually our desires will appear in some form.

After many years, my first marriage came to an end. I had created a void to be filled. Nita appeared in my life, fulfilling all those earlier aspects of a meaningful marital relationship. My intention to find the right marriage partner had been manifested. I believe the key to synchronicity is to pay attention to occurrences around us and never to give up hope.

The more we are aware of synchronicities appearing in our lives, the greater their validation and our trust in them. As we gain more confidence, we give greater power to our intentions. Synchronicity is the affirmation of our creative intentions.

January 15, 2007

WHAT IF...
We were more aware of the power of our intentions?

What if we were more aware of the power of our intentions? I believe we would pay more attention to them. Intentions are the seeds of creation. All that we bring into the world starts with our intentions, and the Universe responds without judgment.

The Universe goes right into action to bring into manifestation whatever we intend. Once we declare our intentions, we need not worry about them. The Universe will take care of the details. Our worries only limit the Universe. We need to recognize and honor that the Universe/Source has much more information and knowledge at its command, and will furnish a better and quicker way to manifest whatever it is that we intend.

The part that we need to play is to feel deserving, and to be open to receiving. When we do not feel deserving of our intentions, we give the Universe mixed messages. Those non-deserving messages will make our intentions null and void. We need to remain open, even as our intentions are being honored and delivered, because they may be manifested in unlikely ways.

Once we have received our intentions, we need to give thanks with gratitude. It is the gratitude that gives the message to the Universe that we are open to receive even more of what we intend. The Universe wants nothing less than to give us all that we ask for. We live in a universe of unlimited abundance.

One of my greatest intentions for many years has been "that the wisest, most benevolent souls have entered my life." It is with gratitude and thanks that I have felt blessed with receiving this intention. I have an abundance of beautiful, wise, and loving people in my life. It is with people like you, and many others, that I feel truly blessed and rich beyond measure. These relationships add great joy to my world.

We can manifest anything we desire with intention. Truly, the Universe delivers abundantly as we use intention to create our greatest dreams and desires.

February 5, 2007

WHAT IF...
We supported each other as though we were One?

What if we supported each other as though we were One? I believe we could experience a new world. It could be a world of abundance for all. All resources could be distributed where the need is the greatest. Our consciousness could be one where we feel the pain and the joy of others. We could seek the equilibrium of balance among all people. The well-being of others becomes a conscious reflection of us while differences are still honored.

Anger can greatly dissipate when everyone and everything is regarded as an interconnected whole. This could bring about fewer feelings of separation and duality. People's feelings and emotions could change from jealousy and resentment to a desire for positive connection. This desire intentionally adds to our own joy and self worth.

When people come together, interacting for the good of the whole, they naturally experience joy and satisfaction in their lives. Feeling connected and loved is what we naturally desire. We already are interconnected with each other and with God/Source. Being fully awake, we act from our highest intention.

As I write these words, I feel this interconnected support. Our spiritual center currently has a "Hope Project" which offers furnishings and other resources to those who, for whatever reason, are starting over in life. When we experience support, we feel valued and hopeful. Through the process of giving and receiving, the energy exchanged makes us feel more loved and connected.

Containing the Divine in our essence, we have that ability to co-create our reality. To a greater degree, we move toward enjoying our experiences by supporting each other. It is about desire, will, and action.

February 12, 2007

WHAT IF...
We paid more attention to our dreams?

What if we paid more attention to our dreams? I believe we could learn so much from them. Our dreams have much to offer us. At the very least, dreams offer us creative experiences. Some dreams give us opportunities to check out different actions we might take in our physical life. Often, repetitive dreams can reveal ongoing issues in our life. Many other dreams are just the body's release of the day's activities and stresses. At first glance, many dreams seem to make no sense at all. If we just take the time to explore our dreams, we could use them to give us direction and answers to many of our life concerns.

Dream experiences have many advantages to further explore ourselves. We can instantly change our actions while in the dream state. We do this without suffering the consequences of those actions, unlike what happens while in our awakened state. As we explore our different dream experiences, we can then choose the best scenario for our awakened life, saving us much time and grief. Dreams can give us much empathy and insights into the world outside ourselves.

I usually remember at least two dreams a night. Dreams that have given me insights include dreams as other life forms. I've had dreams of being a seagull flying with the flock out at sea. I've been a primate, swinging through the trees with ease and grace. I've even had dreams of being on other planets, experiencing an unusual life. Some dreams can even be as expansive as being a point of consciousness moving across the cosmos. These dreams and many others have given me a greater appreciation of all life forms, and the expansiveness of our reality. It has been a conscious decision of mine to explore my dreams, and I invite you to do this too.

I remember my dreams through a number of helpful ways. First, just before I fall asleep, I program myself to remember my dreams when I wake up. If I were to awaken at night in the middle of a dream, I might consciously and emotionally repeat, over and over, the major experience of the dream. In this way I would have a better chance of recalling the dream in the morning. At other times it may be helpful to write down my dreams as soon as I awake. The more awake I become, the greater the chance of losing the dream recall. This is why I feel it is important to capture the dream quickly, upon awakening, and write down some of the main ideas.

Dreams are a part of everyone's life. Everyone dreams; this includes those who have no dream recall. Make a conscious decision to recall your dreams, explore their meanings, and expand your life experiences. This is one way to help live life to the fullest. Maybe life, as we know it, is the real dream.

February 19, 2007

WHAT IF...
We found peace within ourselves?

What if we found peace within ourselves? This is the first step to create peace in our world. We cannot give to the world that which we don't have ourselves. When we have peace within, we contribute peace to the collective whole. We can draw upon that collective peace as we spread it to the manifested world.

First, to have peace within, we need to feel good about ourselves. As humans, we are flawed; yet we do the best we can, given our imperfections. We feel peaceful when we acknowledge our existence as perfect creations in God's image. Unity spiritual teachings state, "We are spiritual beings having a human experience." When we acknowledge the Divinity within us, it becomes easier to find peace and live without fear.

When we live in fear, peace becomes more elusive. Fear brings out the illusions of separation, and separation brings out the fear of lack. Separation creates reactionary responses to real and imaginary issues in our lives. The opposite of fear is love. When we are in a state of love, we become proactive because we are filled with love. We seek to respond to others in a loving way through loving expressions that create peace within.

As years go by, I find myself more and more at

peace. Increased awareness has given me the tools to create a "spiral of being," or state of inner peace. The more peaceful I feel, the more loving and responsive I am to others.

We are living at a time of rapidly expanding self-awareness. As we believe in our goodness and claim our power, it becomes easier to find peace within. Peace is our natural state of being. Let us be the peace that we want to see in our world.

February 26, 2007

WHAT IF...
We lived life from a nonjudgmental perspective?

What if we lived life from a nonjudgmental perspective? I believe the more nonjudgmental we are, the easier it becomes to experience Oneness. Whenever we come from a place of judgment, we create a sense of separation. Judgment of others usually tells more about us than the people we are judging. The more judgmental we are, the more our ego has control.

Our ego wants us to feel superior through judgment of others. One example of judgment is demeaning someone else's belief to justify our actions and self-worth. The more aware, and in control of our ego we become, the less need we have to judge others. It's a win-win situation all around.

We can never fully understand another person. We know that each person's soul has a purpose, and that purpose can be quite complicated. It can involve a soul's journey that covers many lifetimes and experiences. It may involve karma or other repercussions from the universal law of cause and effect. Only God and the person truly know the reasons leading to specific actions.

When we live without judgment, we are honoring and expressing respect for others. It is another way of acknowledging the perfection and Divinity of all life.

This also allows us to feel connected to others. Indeed, it is a celebratory achievement when we realize that we have developed a pattern of genuine nonjudgment of others and of ourselves.

In my own life's journey, certain actions I've taken could easily have been judged by others. Only I fully know how my actions affect my soul's purpose. At peace with the choices I have made in life, I've gained greater awareness. Over time, I have become less judgmental, and this is very liberating.

As humans, it is very difficult *not* to be judgmental. Judgment may be one of the ego's greatest tools in support of its own recognition and existence. With effort and self-awareness, we can achieve a nonjudgmental attitude. The rewards will bring a greater sense of peace and unity to our lives. We are One in this world.

March 5, 2007

WHAT IF...
We responded to life with open minds?

What if we responded to life with open minds? This would allow unlimited awareness to enter our consciousness. Life would have much potential and our growth could catapult us in ways we could not imagine. We truly could become the expansive co-creators that we were meant to be.

As children, we come into the world with an open mind. It is only through limiting messages from other people and resulting subsequent life experiences that we begin limiting our belief systems and our creative abilities. We incrementally close our minds with each hurt and wound we encounter.

Soon these experiences become a self-fulfilling prophecy. By the time most of us are young adults, we have unknowingly surrendered to restricted belief systems and potential. We want to fit in and feel comfortable in our social surroundings. To do so usually requires that we buy into family and community belief systems and viewpoints. This is one price we pay for conformity. How could we have known?

Eventually, most of us become strong enough to be mature and confident in our viewpoints. It is then that we are able to see beyond those restricted perceptions. Open minds are very freeing and empowering. Never in human history has there been a better time to cultivate open minds. A sudden increase of new knowledge and awareness is available to our human consciousness. We are becoming multidimensional beings, with unlimited potential, as we gain greater awareness and create new experiences.

I have never lost that curiosity and open-mindedness of a child. This is a blessing because I have been able to expand my mind and experience many wonders. My greatest thrill is the anticipation of what lies ahead. The future just keeps getting better and better. Life is an open-ended puzzle. As more of the puzzle pieces of life fit together, the puzzle borders keep expanding. There is no end to the expansion.

Are we willing to let go of the security of feeling safe and accepted so that we might become more open-minded? Society rarely accepts new ideas, beliefs, and knowledge without some criticism, yet it is those very ideas that could change our world and our reality. The world is exponentially changing. We need to get on board, be more open-minded, and aspire to our greatest visions. Now is the time to be bold co-creators of change.

March 12, 2007

WHAT IF...
We tolerated all paths to God?

What if we tolerated all paths to God? I believe we would come to a greater appreciation, acceptance and understanding of others. Some wars and other forms of hostilities could be avoided, and everyone could gain from this tolerance in so many ways.

It has been said that different paths to God/Source are like climbing a mountain. God is at the top of the mountain and there are many paths to the summit. I was raised in a traditional organized religion that represents one of these paths. As I grew up, I started to acknowledge that other paths also had answers that led to a greater understanding of God. Eventually, I found that my traditional path was too limiting and restricted, so I left that beaten path, wandered around, and searched for my own path.

I took flight. From my aerial view of the mountain, I was able to see that all paths led to the mountain peak. Some paths were smoother, others rockier, and some more winding, yet they all led to the top. From my viewpoint, I realized that it wasn't the path that was important, but the journey itself. Even people who follow the same path don't step in the same places along the path. Each of us experiences what we believe is the best path although our path may be very different from the paths of others. We may be confident that the path we have chosen is just right for us.

How we interact with others along the journey is more important than the path itself. The more we assist each other along the journey, the easier and greater is our experience. Eventually, we will reach the mountaintop. Once we come to that peak, we will gather together to discuss the journey and our experiences along the way. Which path we took will be of little consequence compared to the realization that we are all seekers and a part of the mountain.

Acknowledging this, let us be more tolerant of individuals' paths to God. We cannot walk in their shoes, but we can assist them along the way. They, in turn, can assist us. It is how we conduct our journey that is important. The goal for all of us is the same—conscious and continuous union with God/Source.

March 19, 2007

WHAT IF...
We took some time to "smell the roses"?

What if we took time to smell the roses? When we take time to slow down and appreciate the little things in life, we reduce our stress and anxiety levels. We focus on things in the present moment and start to see our interconnection with all of life. We may realize what a wonderful world we live in and how blessed we are.

There are many ways to "smell the roses." We can go out into nature and marvel at the life rhythms of other creatures. This can be anything from studying moss growing under a log to observing a flock of migrating waterfowl heading north to their annual breeding grounds. A walk in the woods on a sunny, spring day may fill us with wonder, bringing us back into the moment. We will feel relaxed and uplifted when we pause long enough from our racing thoughtstoseethebeautyandtheintriguingdetailsofnature.

We may like to turn our attention to young children as another way to "smell the roses." Young children live in the moment with their days full of curiosity and wonder. We can let go of our imagined worries and concerns (even if it is just for a short period of time) when we take time to play with a child. Spending time with a carefree child helps us to remember, once again, our carefree selves.

We can take time to "smell the roses" by pursuing

creative activities. I have a number of such outlets. I enjoy creating oil paintings of nature and scenery in the winter months. As the earth comes alive again in the spring, I become One with our flower and vegetable gardens, enjoying everything about them. It is inspiring to partner with the Universe by working the soil in my hands at the beginning of the season, by continuous plant nurturing throughout the season, and by picking raspberries in the cool summer evening breezes and completing the harvest.

As I slow down, becoming present in the moment, I learn to appreciate everything in my life. One of my favorite moments is to relax in the early morning with a cup of coffee, talking to my wife about anything and everything. This is a reflective, meditative, and positive time for both of us.

We need to be good to ourselves. Take time to "smell the roses." As we do, we'll feel better, and we'll appreciate a greater connection to life.

March 26, 2007

WHAT IF...
We were visited by beings from other worlds?

What if we were visited by beings from other worlds? Accepting this concept shouldn't be too much of a stretch for most of us. I recently read that the majority of the population believes in UFO's. Society leaders, however, will not outwardly acknowledge any evidence. As we become more spiritually aware and mature, it is timely for us to expand our thinking to include the cosmos. It is ridiculous to believe that humans are the only intelligent life form in our vast universe.

As a human race, we need to be honest about how far we have advanced. Creating war or destroying a planet out of greed and ignorance are not routes that superior civilizations would take. Highly-developed beings, in other parts of the universe, might think twice about becoming involved with us at our current stage of maturity. Hopefully, this will change. We need to become an interconnected, global community that honors all life everywhere.

I know of several people who claim to communicate with more evolved beings from other worlds using telepathy or channeling. Physical sightings of UFO ships have been recorded throughout history. Even today it is not that uncommon to hear about such sightings. I truly believe that we will begin to see more and more evidence of extraterrestrials.

Are we afraid to acknowledge that more advanced beings could exist in our universe? Maybe this acknowledgment would alter our comfortable sense of reality. I believe we are in an exciting period of history in which our sense of reality is changing. Some of us are more open to this than others. As the human race continues to evolve (and I believe it will), I wouldn't be surprised if other intelligent life forms find increasingly more tangible ways to connect with us.

What might that mean? Their advanced technologies and spiritual wisdom might assist us in overcoming many of our current global problems. Maybe they are just waiting for us to ask for their assistance. If we are truly all One, why not be open to a more expansive reality that includes our cosmic neighbors? The positive outcome could be that our lives would become richer and more productive. An even more significant outcome is that they might assist us in saving our planet. Of course we should not wait for them to save us, but appreciate any advanced assistance.

Perhaps, it is up to us. Do we want to see an expansive picture and be less self-absorbed? Are we willing to connect with other intelligent life, or are we continuing to think we are the center of the universe? When we maintain a narrow view of ourselves, we limit our possibilities. Please join me in encouraging the appearance of our spiritual cosmic brothers and sisters by affirming only positive outcomes. The affirmation, "That which we focus on, we attract" helps us overcome our fears.

March 9, 2009

WHAT IF...
We ...?

For real changes to occur, the world we want to create needs to be envisioned by a significant number of people. Since it is important to the whole for you to add your vision of a new world, I left the last "WHAT IF..." entry for you to title and complete. We are all One. The world needs your input. What does your vision for a peaceful, interdependent, harmonious earth look like?

Thoughts on Reality

Thoughts on Reality: An Outline

It has been said: If you cannot find the book you want to read, then you must write it yourself. I've always wanted to know: *What is reality?* Unable to find a book exclusively dedicated to the subject, I decided years ago to keep a list of ideas that could be used as a possible framework to develop the topic. Here I share an overview of multiple realities.

Levels of Reality in Relation to Oneness

Section 1: Physical Dimension, Lowest Level of Reality
Section 2: Higher Dimensions, Higher Levels of Reality
        (How to Connect)
Section 3: Dimensions in Reality, Levels of Awareness
Section 4: Space, Time
Section 5: Unity, Oneness
Section 6: Love, God

Section 1: Physical Dimension, Lowest Level of Reality

    A. Means to understand our reality

        2. Physics, including Quantum Physics

        3. Eastern, Western philosophy

    B. Connections with the higher dimensions in the physical plane

        1. Incarnated spiritual beings, including Jesus, Buddha and others

        2. Apparitions

            a. Marian and other higher level entities from the celestial plane

            b. Incarnated and ethereal spiritual friends, relatives trying to connect with those in the physical plane

            c. Ethereal, spiritual beings caught in the lower levels of vibration of the astral plane

    C. UFO's

        1. Visitation from higher-level entities from this dimension as well as from higher dimensions

        2. Curious entities from other solar systems and galaxies in this dimension

Section 2: Higher Dimensions, Higher Levels of Reality (How to Connect)

    A. Meditation: transcendental, yoga, and prayer

    B. Near-Death experience

    C. Out-of-Body Experience

    D. Dream state, including lucid dreams

    E. Intuition

    F. Self-hypnosis

    G. Channeling

Section 3: Dimensions in Reality, Levels of Awareness

    A. Energy as a vibration that includes love, light, and thought

        1. Love, including the form of healing energy

        2. Light, in connection to higher dimensions (in a higher vibration, our consciousness takes the form of light energy)

        3. Thought

            a. "We are that which watches our thoughts pass through our mind"

            b. Ways in which it creates reality in and out of time

            c. Its source and power

                1. The power of belief

                2. The power of choice

B. Energy at different vibrations changes the dimension in reality

C. As vibration increases, the intensity of Oneness increases

Section 4: Space, Time

A. Eternal now vs. linear time

1. Means to experience the eternal now

2. An understanding of linear time in the physical world vs. time in the Eternal Now

3. Linear time can only be experienced in the lowest vibration, physical reality

B. Issues dealing with space, time

1. Mystics/Prophets and prophesy

2. Astrologers, astrology

3. Psychics, premonitions

C. Reincarnation

1. How we live many lifetimes, yet how they all occur at the same time

2. Soul mates, soul companions

Section 5: Unity, Oneness

A. There is no separation in reality; everything is a part of the oneness of God

1. The Godhead is the source of all that is

2. Everything that ascends, converges

3. The higher the vibration, the greater the experience and reality of love
   a. Love and all of its forms are the highest vibration
   b. Fear, and all of its forms are the lowest vibration

B. Reality vs. Illusion
   1. Means of achieving and experiencing reality
      a. Love, the only reality there truly is, can be expressed in many forms, including wisdom and knowledge
         1. Loving yourself, acknowledging and accepting your divinity
         2. Being of service to all others
         3. Being creative, as a co-creator with God
      b. Forgiveness
      c. Living in the eternal now
      d. Synchronicity
      e. Joy
   2. The experience of illusion
      a. Ego, belief of separation
      b. Fear, all of its forms and ramifications
      c. Belief that we are in our body instead of our body is in us

    d. Misunderstanding of good and evil

Section 6: Love, God
    A. Ecstasy
    B. Inner ocean of silence

Selected Reading

Selected Reading

Many authors have given me great insights, and their ideas have helped humanity to grow and change. This book list is by no means a complete record of all of the works and sources I have consulted; however, it represents the range of reading on which I have based my ideas. I offer selected authors and titles and have categorized the books by related topics. I hope that you also will find these books helpful and enlightening as you follow your spiritual path.

Channeling/Psychic Abilities

Broody Jr., Theodore A. *Ascension — Beginner's Manual.* 1989.
Broody Jr., Theodore A. *The Brotherhood of Intuition.* 1987.
Bartholomew (Disciple) as channeled through Mary-Margaret Moore. *Bartholomew: Reflections of an Elder Brother — Awakening from the Dream.* 1989.
Bartholomew (Disciple) as channeled through Mary-Margaret Moore. *I Come as a Brother, A Remembrance of Illusions.* 1986.

Basil, Robert. *Not Necessarily the New Age: Critical Essays.* 1988.

Cannnon, Dolores. *Jesus and the Essenes.* 1992.

Carroll, Lee. *The New Energy Apocalypse.* 2007.

Carroll, Lee. *Kryon Book 10 — A New Dispensation.* 2004.

Carroll, Lee. *Kryon Book 9 — The New Beginning (2000 And Beyond).* 2002.

Carroll, Lee. *Kryon Book 8 — 2000 Passing the Marker (Understanding the New Millennium Energy).* 2000.

Cayce, Edgar Evans. *Edgar Cayce on Atlantis.* 1968.

Christ, The. *New Teachings — For an Awakening Humanity.* 1986.

Ferguson, Marilyn. *The Aquarium Conspiracy — Personal and Social Transformation in the 1980s.* 1980.

Grabhorn, Lynn. *Planet Two — Earth in a Higher Dimension...Are You Ready?* 2004.

Herman, Ronna. *On Wings of Light — Messages of Hope and Inspiration from Archangel Michael.* 1996.

Hicks, Ester and Jerry. *Ask and it is Given — Learning to Manifest Your Desires.* 2004.

Kilmo, John. *Channeling Investigations from Paranormal Sources.* 1987.

Kilmo, John. *Synchronicity — the Bridge Between Matter and Mind.* 1987.

Magdalena, Flo Aeveia. *I Remember Union — The Story of Mary Magdalena.* 1992.

Marciniak, Barbara. *Family of Light*. 1999.

Marciniak, Barbara. *The Bringers of the Dawn — Teachings from the Pleiadians*. 1992.

McMoneagle, Joseph. *Remote Viewing Secrets — A Handbook*. 2000.

Montgomery, Ruth. *Herald in the New Age*. 1986.

Montgomery, Ruth. *Strangers Among Us*. 1979.

Redfield, James. *The Celestine Prophecy — An Experimental Guide*. 1995.

Redfield, James. *The Celestine Prophecy*. 1993.

Renard, Gary R, *The Disappearance of the Universe*. 2004.

Roads, Michael J. *Getting There*. 1998.

Roberts, Jane. *Dreams, Evolution and Value Fulfillment — Vol. 1, 2*. 1986.

Roman, Sanaya. *Opening to Channel: How to Connect with Your Guide*. 1987.

Rother, Steve, and the Group and Barbara Rother. *Greetings from Home*. 2006.

Rother, Steve and the Group. *Welcome Home — The New Planet Earth*. 2002.

Rother, Steve and the Group. *Re-Member*. 2000.

Solara. *11:11 Inside the Doorway*. 1996.

Stibal, Vianna. *Go Up and Work With God*. 2000.

Stone, Ph.D., Joshua David. *The Complete Ascension Manual — How to Achieve Ascension in this Lifetime*. 1994.

Tarig, Harary, & Sheman. *The Mind Race: Understanding and Using Psychic Abilities.* 1984.

Vaughan, Alan. *Incredible Coincidence: The Baffling World of Synchronicity.* 1979.

Walsch, Neale Donald. *Tomorrow's God—Our Greatest Spiritual Challenge.* 2004.

Walsch, Neale Donald. *Questions and Answers on Conversations with God.* 1999.

Walsch, Neale Donald. *Conversations With God—Book 3.* 1998.

Marian Apparitions

Connell, Ian. *Queen of the Cosmos—Interviews with the Visionaries of Medjugorje.* 1990.

Craig, Mary. *Spark from Heaven—The Mystery of the Madonna of Medjugorje.* 1988.

Laurentin, René. *The Apparitions at Medjugorje Prolonged.* 1985.

Pelletier, Joseph. *The Queen of Peace Visits Medjugorje.* 1985.

Weible, Wayne. *Letters From Medjugorje.* 1991.

Modern Physics

Braden, Greg. *Awakening to Zero Point—The Collective Initiation.* 1997.

Calder, Nigel. *Einstein's Universe.* 1979.

Capra, Fritjof. *The Tao of Physics—An Exploration of the Parallels between Modern Physics and Eastern Mysticism.* 2000.

Davies, P.C.W., and J. Brown. *Superstrings—The Theory of Everything.* 1988.

Hawking, Steven. *A Brief History of Time.* 1988.

Hawking, Steven. *The Universe in a Nutshell.* 2001.

Kaku, Michio. *Hyperspace: A Scientific Odyssey Through Parallel Universes, Time Warps, and the Tenth Dimension.* 1994.

Steiger, Brad. *Worlds Before Our Own.* 1978.

Student of the Wisdom Teachings. *Our Conscious Universe + Mysteries Thereof.* 1998.

Talbot, Michael. *Mysticism and the New Physics.* 1981.

Talbot, Michael. *Beyond the Quantum.* 1981.

Weber, Renee. *Dialogs with Scientists and Sages: The Search for Unity.* 1986.

Wolf, Fred Alan. *Parallel Universes.* 1988.

Wolf, Fred Alan. *Star Wave: Mind, Consciousness, and Quantum Physics.* 1984.

Wolf, Fred Alan. *Taking the Quantum Leap: New Physics for Non Scientists.* 1981.

Zohar & Marshall. *The Quantum Self: Human Nature and Consciousness Defined by the New Modern Physics.* 1990.

Zukav, Gary. *The Dancing Wuli Master: An Overview of the New Physics.* 1979.

Near Death Experiences/Reincarnation/Life Beyond Death

Atwater & Kirkwood. *Beyond the Light: What Isn't Being Said About Near-Death Experiences.* 1994.

Curie, Ian. *You Cannot Die—The Incredible Findings of a Century of Research on Death.* 1978.

Eadie, Betty. *Embraced by the Light.* 1992.

Holmes M.D., Jesse Herman, and the Holmes Research Team. *As We See It from Here.* 1980.

Holzer, Hans. *Born Again: The Truth About Reincarnation.* 1970.

Martin & Romanowski. *We Don't Die: George Anderson's Conversations with the Other Side.* 1988.

Moody, Raymond. *Coming Back: A Psychiatrist Explores Past Life Journeys.* 1990.

Morse & Perry. *Transformed by the Light: The Powerful Effect of Near-Death Experiences on People's Lives.* 1992.

Morse & Perry. *Closer to the Light: Learning from the Near-Death Experiences of Children.* 1990.

Newton, Ph.D., Michael. *Journey of Souls — Case Studies of Life between Lives.* 1997.

Ring, Keith. *Heading Towards Omega: In Search of the Meaning of the Near Death Experience.* 1984.

Van Praagh, James. *Talking to Heaven — A Medium's Message of Life After Death.* 1997.

Wilson, Ian. *The After Death Experience: The Physics of the Non-Physical.* 1987.

Out-of-Body Experiences/Dreaming

Black, David. *Ekstasy: Out-of-Body Experiences.* 1975.

Crookall, Robert. *Mechanisms of Astral Projection.* 1968.

Dillard & Krippher. *Deamworking: How to Use Your Dreams for Creative Problem-Solving.* 1988.

LaBerge & Rheingold. *Exploring the World of Lucid Dreaming.* 1990.

Monroe, Robert. *Ultimate Journey.* 1994.

Monroe, Robert. *Far Journeys (on Out of the Body Experiences).* 1985.

Monroe, Robert. *Journeys Out of the Body.* 1977.

Powell, Authur. *The Astral Body and Other Astral Phenomena.* 1982.

Stack, Rick. *Out-of-Body Adventures: 30 Days to the Most Exciting Experiences of Your Life.* 1988.

Philosophies/Meditation

Achad, Frater. *Melchizedek Truth Principles—From the Ancient Mystical White Brotherhood.* 1988.

Achad, Frater. *The Ancient Mystical White Brotherhood.* 1987.

Callahan, John D. *Science and Christianity.* 1986.

Chopra, Deepak. *How to Know God—The Soul's Journey Into the Mystery of Mysteries.* 2000.

Chopra, Deepak. *The Path to Love—Renewing the Power of Spirit in Your Life.* 1997.

Dyer, Dr. Wayne W. *Change Your Thoughts—Change Your Life: Living the Wisdom of the Tao.* 2007.

Dyer, Dr. Wayne W. *Your Sacred Self—Making the Decision to be Free.* 1995.

Dubos, Rene. *A God Within.* 1972.

Findhorn Community. *The Findhorn Community: Pioneering a New Vision of Man and Nature in Cooperation.* 1975.

Foundation for Inner Peace. *A Course In Miracles.* 1975.

Frankl, Viktor E. *Man's Search for Meaning.* 1984.

Hayward, Jeremy. *Perceiving Ordinary Magic: Science and Intuitive Wisdom.* 1985.

Holmes, Ernest. *The Science of Minds — A Philosophy, a Faith, a Way of Life.* 1938.

Jung, Carl. *Man and His Symbols.* 1964.

Karppinski, Gloria. *Where Two Worlds Touch: Spiritual Rites of Passage.* 1990.

Kelly, Mary. *The Fireside Treasury of Light: An Anthology of the Best in New Age Literature.* 1990.

Laski, Marghanita. *Ecstasy In Secular and Religious Experiences.* 1990.

Lucas, Mary and Ellen. *Teilhard: The Man, the Priest, the Scientist.* 1977.

Maclaine, Shirley. *Awakening Intuition.* 1979.

McFadden, Steven. *Profiles in Wisdom: Native Elders Speak About the Earth.* 1991.

Modi, Shahuntala. *Memories of God and Creation: Remembering from the Subconscious Mind.* 2000.

Morgan, Michael. *Mutant Message Down Under.* 1991.

Roads, Michael J. *Journey Into Oneness.* 1994.

Roads, Michael J. *Journey Into Nature.* 1990.

Roads, Michael J. *Talking With Nature.* 1985.

Thurston, Mark. *The Inner Power of Silence: A Universal Way of Meditation.* 1986.

Skutch, Robert. *Journey Without Distance: The Story Behind the Course in Miracles.* 1984.

Zukav, Gary and Linda Francis. *The Heart of the Soul — Emotional Awareness.* 2001.

Prophesy

Bryce, Sheradon. *Joy Riding the Universe*. 1993.

Hogue, John. *Predictions of the Future—Nostradamus and the Millennium*. 1987.

Hunt, Dave. *Peace Prosperity and the Coming Holocaust*. 1977.

Montgomery, Ruth. *The World to Come—The Guides Long-Awaited Predictions for the Dawning Age*. 1999.

Rain, Mary Summer. *Phoenix Rising—No-Eyes Vision of the Changes to Come*. 1987.

Snow, Ph.D., Chet B. *Mass Dreams of the Future*. 1989.

Spaulding, Baird. *Life and Teaching of the Master of the Far East, Vol. 1-5*. 1976.

Wilde, Stuart. *Whispering Winds of Change—Perceptions of a New World*. 1993.

Self-Help/Psychology

Altea, Rosemary. *Proud Spirit—Lessons, Insights, and Healing from 'The Voices of the Spirit World.'* 1997.

Altea, Rosemary. *The Eagle and the Rose*. 1995.

Ardagh, Arjauna. *Awakening Into Oneness*. 2007.

Armstrong, Herbert. *The Incredible Human Potential*. 1978.

Bloomfield M.D., H. and R. Kory. *Happiness*. 1976.

Burroughs, Tony. *The Code — 10 Intentions for a Better World.* 2008

Carnegie, Dale. *How to Stop Worrying and Start Living.* 1975.

Cedercrans, Lucille. *Creative Thinking.* 2001.

Chopra, M.D., Deepak. *The Seven Spiritual Laws of Success.* 1994.

Chopra, M.D., Deepak. *Ageless Body, Timeless Mind – The Quantum Alternative to Growing Old.* 1993.

Cohen, Alan. *I Had It All the Time.* 1995.

Covey, Stephen. *The 7 Habits of Highly Effective People.* 1989.

Gawain, Shakti & King. *Living in the Light.* 1986.

Hawkins, M.D., Ph.D., David R. *Power vs. Force – The Hidden Determinants of Human Behavior.* 2002.

Hay, Louise L. *You Can Heal Your Life.* 1987.

Jampolsky, Gerald. *Love is the Answer: Creating Positive Relationships.* 1990.

Jampolsky, Gerald. *Change Your Mind, Change Your Life.* 1993.

Mandino, Og. *The Choice.* 1984.

McFaden, Steven. *Ancient Voices-Current Affairs: The Legend of the Rainbow Warriors.* 1992.

Milan, Patrick. *Inspiration Point.* 2008.

Moore, Thomas. *Soul Mates: Honoring the Mysteries of Love and Relationships.* 1994.

Myss, Caroline. *Entering the Castle – Finding the Inner Path to God and Your Soul's Purpose.* 2007.

Peale, Norman Vincent. *The Power of Positive Thinking.* 1976.

Peck, Scott M. *A World Waiting to be Born.* 1993.

Peck, Scott M. *The Road Less Traveled.* 1978.

Powell, John. *The Secret of Staying in Love.* 1974.

Rasha, received by. *Oneness – The Teaching.* 2003.

Ray, Ph.D., Paul H., and Sherry R. Anderson. *The Cultural Creatives – How 50 Million People Are Changing the World.* 2000.

Rother, Steve. *Spiritual Psychology – The Twelve Primary Life Lessons.* 2004.

Singh, Tara. *Channeling: How to Reach Your Spirit Guides.* 1988.

Tolle, Eckhart. *A New Earth – Awakening to Your Life's Purpose.* 2005.

Tolle, Eckhart. *The Power of Now – A Guide to Spiritual Enlightenment.* 1999.

Williamson, Marianne. *Everyday Grace – Having Hope, Finding Forgiveness, and Making Miracles.* 2002.

Williamson, Marianne. *A Return to Love: Reflections on the Principles of a Course in Miracles.* 1992.

Zukav, Gary. *The Seat of the Soul.* 1990.

UFO's

Brownell, Winifred S. *UFO's Key to Earth Destiny*. 1980.

Carey, Ken. *Return of the Bird Tribes*. 1988.

Carey, Ken. *Star Seed – The Third Millennium*. 1991.

Ouspensky, P.D. *In Search of the Miraculous: Fragments of an Unknown Teaching*. 1976.

Weed, Joseph. *Date with the Gods*. 1986.